Ben Stacy Jerrik (Ed.)

Computer Usage Company

Ben Stacy Jerrik (Ed.)

Computer Usage Company

Software, Federal Aviation Administration, National Aviation Facilities Experimental Center

Part Press

Imprint

Permission is granted to copy, distribute and/or modify this document under the terms of the GNU Free Documentation License, Version 1.2 or any later version published by the Free Software Foundation; with no Invariant Sections, with the Front-Cover Texts, and with the Back- Cover Texts. A copy of the license is included in the section entitled "GNU Free Documentation License".

All parts of this book are extracted from Wikipedia, the free encyclopedia (www.wikipedia.org).

You can get detailed informations about the authors of this collection of articles at the end of this book. The editors (Ed.) of this book are no authors. They have not modified or extended the original texts.

Pictures published in this book can be under different licences than the GNU Free Documentation License. You can get detailed informations about the authors and licences of pictures at the end of this book.

The content of this book was generated collaboratively by volunteers. Please be advised that nothing found here has necessarily been reviewed by people with the expertise required to provide you with complete, accurate or reliable information. Some information in this book maybe misleading or wrong. The Publisher does not guarantee the validity of the information found here. If you need specific advice (f.e. in fields of medical, legal, financial, or risk management questions) please contact a professional who is licensed or knowledgeable in that area.

Any brand names and product names mentioned in this book are subject to trademark, brand or patent protection and are trademarks or registered trademarks of their respective holders. The use of brand names, product names, common names, trade names, product descriptions etc. even without a particular marking in this works is in no way to be construed to mean that such names may be regarded as unrestricted in respect of trademark and brand protection legislation and could thus be used by anyone.

Cover image: www.ingimage.com
Concerning the licence of the cover image please contact ingimage.

Publisher:
Part Press is a trademark of
International Book Market Service Ltd., 17 Rue Meldrum, Beau Bassin, 1713-01 Mauritius
Email: info@bookmarketservice.com
Website: www.bookmarketservice.com

Published in 2012

Printed in: U.S.A., U.K., Germany. This book was not produced in Mauritius.

ISBN: 978-613-6-26749-4

Contents

Articles

References

Computer_Usage_Company

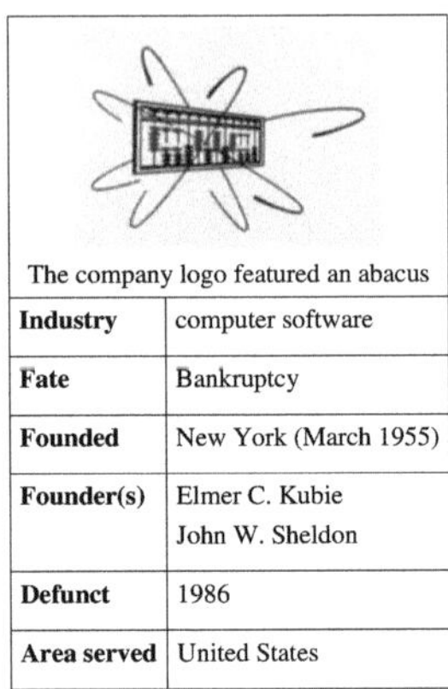

The company logo featured an abacus

Industry	computer software
Fate	Bankruptcy
Founded	New York (March 1955)
Founder(s)	Elmer C. Kubie John W. Sheldon
Defunct	1986
Area served	United States

Computer Usage Company (1955–1986), sometimes called **Computer Usage Corporation**, was the first independent company to market computer software.

History

Computer Usage Company (CUC) was founded in March 1955 by Elmer C. Kubie (1926–2004[1]) and John W. Sheldon. They had formerly worked together at IBM, and planned to offer services to help develop computer programs. The initial investment of US$40,000 supported the founders and a staff of five.[2] Although the term software had been coined earlier as a prank, it did not appear in print until later.[3] Before this time, software was developed either by the users of the computers, or the few commercial computer vendors of the time. CUC is generally considered the first company to develop software independently.[4] [5] [6] CUC's first project was a program written for California Research Corporation to simulate the flow of oil.[7] The first offices were located in New York city. On October 3, 1955 Computer Usage Company, Inc. was incorporated in Delaware. George R. Trimble, Jr. became Corporate Technical Director in February 1956 after work on the IBM 650. Trimble headed a project to computerize the air traffic control system of the Federal Aviation Administration. This work was done at the National Aviation Facilities Experimental Center in New Jersey.[8]

In 1959 an office in Washington, DC was opened, since CUC had business with the US Navy. In April 1960 the company had an Initial Public Offering of stock shares, and grew to three managers, 37 mathematicians, 6 physicists, and 3 engineers.[9] Later in 1960 CUC established a division to sell computer time and in Spring 1961 opened an office in Los Angeles.[10] Cuthbert Hurd joined the company as chairman in 1962, a former division director from IBM.[11]

The FAA was planning to use the IBM 9020 model of the new IBM System/360, so contracted with CUC to develop a compiler for the JOVIAL computer language. The compiler was first developed on a simulator using the IBM 7030 before actual hardware was available. In early 1964, CUC developed software used by CBS Television to track the election results. Sheldon left later in 1964. Another major contract was to implement part of IBM's first time-sharing system, TSS/360. CUC was asked to manage the TSS project, as it was seen as losing ground to competitors in time-sharing. Realizing that performance would never meet expectations, CUC declined.[12] In 1965 the Computer Usage Education subsidiary was formed, headed by Ascher Opler, which published software books and offered courses. One of its best sellers was on Programming the IBM system/360.[13] Carl H. Reynolds joined as President of the new Computer Usage Development Company subsidiary in 1966. Reynolds had been director of programming for the Data Systems Division of IBM during the development of the System/360.[14]

By 1967 CUC had a staff of over 700 people in 12 offices and revenues over $13 million. An office in Dallas, Texas was established to work on a contract with Texas Instruments to develop software including an operating system and a FORTRAN compiler for the TI Advanced Scientific Computer.[8] During that time, the company's vice president was H. Dean Brown. Kubie and Reynolds left in July 1968 and the company changed direction under new president Charles Benton, Jr. from IBM's Federal Systems Division.[15] Benton hired sales people instead of technical people, and contracts did not keep up with overhead.[12]

CUC declared its first loss as a public company in 1969. Other competitors such as Computer Sciences Corporation were now larger. Sears announced they were in discussions for an acquisition, but talks fell through.[16] By early 1970 Benton resigned and Hurd stepped in as president, although he lived in California. Other potential mergers were discussed, including Ross Perot who by now had founded his own service business Electronic Data Systems.[12] CUC negotiated a contract to manage computer facilities at the Firemans Fund Insurance Company, which restored profitability for a time. Hurd left in 1974. Victor Bartoletti became president, but died in 1984 and George C. Strohl from Bank of America became president. However, losses continued to mount as the computer business was now very different from the field dominated by IBM 30 years earlier. By 1985, CUC lost $2.4 million on revenues of only $1.5 million. In 1986 CUC declared bankruptcy and was liquidated in what is known as Chapter 7.[17]

See also

- software industry
- History of IBM

References

[1] http://www.faqs.org/people-search/kubie/

[2] Elmer C. Kubie (Summer 1994). "Recollections of the first software company". *IEEE Annals of the History of Computing* (IEEE Computer Society) **16** (2): 65–71. doi:10.1109/85.279238.

[3] Paul Niquette (1995). "Softword: Provenance for the Word 'Software'" (http://www.niquette.com/books/softword/tocsoft.html). . adapted from *Sophisticated: The Magazine* ISBN 1-58922-233-4

[4] James W. Cortada (January 1996). *Second bibliographic guide to the history of computing, computers, and the information processing industry* (http://books.google.com/books?id=cUxDqNb9smQC&pg=PA27). Greenwood Publishing Group. p. 27. ISBN 9780313295423. .

[5] Eric G. Swedin; David L. Ferro (2007). *Computers: The Life Story of a Technology* (http://books.google.com/books?id=aeekluUpc7kC&pg=PA60). JHU Press. p. 60. ISBN 9780801887741. .

[6] Denise Tsang (October 30, 2006). *The entrepreneurial culture: network advantage within Chinese and Irish software firms* (http://books.google.com/books?id=eae600nls7UC&pg=PA25). Edward Elgar Publishing. p. 25. ISBN 9781845420147. .

[7] "Computer Usage Corporation (CUC)" (http://www.softwarehistory.org/history/cuc.html). *Computer Museum web site*. . Retrieved May 29, 2010.

[8] George R. Trimble Jr. (June 24, 2005). "CUC History" (http://corphist.computerhistory.org/corphist/documents/doc-437a4a92bbf21.doc). Computer History Museum. . Retrieved May 30, 2010.

[9] John H. Gribbin (1960). *Industrial research laboratories of the United States* (http://books.google.com/books?id=pzgrAAAAYAAJ&pg=PA120) (11th ed.). National Academies. p. 120. NAP:14698. .

[10] "Annual Report 1961" (http://archive.computerhistory.org/resources/text/Computer_Usage_Company/cuc.annual_report.1961.102651923.pdf). Computer Usage Company. .

[11] John A. N. Lee (1995). "Cuthbert C. Hurd" (http://books.google.com/books?id=ocx4Jc12mkgC&pg=PA388). *International biographical dictionary of computer pioneers*. Taylor & Francis for IEEE Computer Society Press. pp. 388–389. ISBN 9781884964473. .

[12] Charles R. Fillerup (August 28, 1995). "An Interview with Cuthbert C. Hurd" (http://purl.umn.edu/107371). Charles Babbage Institute, University of Minnesota. . Retrieved May 29, 2010.

[13] Computer Usage Company (1966). Ascher Opler. ed. *Programming the IBM system/360* (http://books.google.com/books?id=NRg1AAAAIAAJ). Wiley. ISBN 0471167053. .

[14] Emerson W. Pugh; Lyle R. Johnson; John H. Palmer (January 4, 1991). *IBM's 360 and early 370 systems* (http://books.google.com/books?id=MFGj_PT_clIC&pg=PA303). MIT Press. p. 303. ISBN 9780262161237. .

[15] "Charles Benton, Jr. Elected President of CUC" (http://archive.computerhistory.org/resources/text/Computer_Usage_Company/070910_download/computerusagecompany.cu_bits_1968_jul/computerusagecompany.cu_bits_1968_jul.pdf). *CU/Bits* (Computer Usage

Corporation). . Retrieved May 29, 2010.

[16] Hammer, Alexander R. (November 1, 1969). "Sears Is Seeking Computer Company; Acquisitions and Combinations Are Planned by Corporations" (http://select.nytimes.com/gst/abstract.html?res=F40F16F93B551B7B93C3A9178AD95F4D8685F9). *New York Times*. . Retrieved May 29, 2010.

[17] Detlev J. Hoch (2000). *Secrets of software success: management insights from 100 software firms around the world* (http://books.google. com/books?id=FPMpZ2qMkKwC&pg=PA37). Harvard Business Press. pp. 37–38. ISBN 9781578511051. .

Further reading

- George R. Trimble Jr. (Summer 2001). "A brief history of computing. Memoirs of living on the edge". *IEEE Annals of the History of Computing* (IEEE Computer Society) **23** (3): 44–59. doi:10.1109/85.948905.
- Luanne (James) Johnson (Summer 1998). "A View From the 1960s: How the Software Industry Began". *IEEE Annals of the History of Computing* (IEEE Computer Society) **20** (1): 36–42. doi:10.1109/85.646207.

Software

Computer software or just **software**, is a collection of computer programs and related data that provides the instructions for telling a computer what to do and how to do it. Software refers to one or more computer programs and data held in the storage of the computer for some purposes. In other words, software is a set of *programs, procedures, algorithms* and its *documentation* concerned with the operation of a data processing system. Program software performs the function of the program it implements, either by directly providing instructions to the computer hardware or by serving as input to another piece of software. The term was coined to contrast to the old term hardware (meaning physical devices). In contrast to hardware, software "cannot be touched".[1] Software is also sometimes used in a more narrow sense, meaning application software only. Sometimes the term includes data that has not traditionally been associated with computers, such as film, tapes, and records.[2]

Computer software is so called to distinguish it from computer hardware, which encompasses the physical interconnections and devices required to store and execute (or run) the software. At the lowest level, executable code consists of machine language instructions specific to an individual processor. A machine language consists of groups of binary values signifying processor instructions that change the state of the computer from its preceding state. Programs are an ordered sequence of instructions for changing the state of the computer in a particular sequence. It is usually written in high-level programming languages that are easier and more efficient for humans to use (closer to natural language) than machine language. High-level languages are compiled or interpreted into machine language object code. Software may also be written in an assembly language, essentially, a mnemonic representation of a machine language using a natural language alphabet. Assembly language must be assembled into object code via an assembler.

History

The first theory about software was proposed by Alan Turing in his 1935 essay *Computable numbers with an application to the Entscheidungsproblem (Decision problem)*.[3] The term "software" was first used in print by John W. Tukey in 1958.[4] Colloquially, the term is often used to mean application software. In computer science and software engineering, software is all information processed by computer system, programs and data.[4] The academic fields studying software are computer science and software engineering.

The history of computer software is most often traced back to the first software bug in 1946. As more and more programs enter the realm of firmware, and the hardware itself becomes smaller, cheaper and faster as predicted by Moore's law, elements of computing first considered to be software, join the ranks of hardware. Most hardware companies today have more software programmers on the payroll than hardware designers, since software tools have automated many tasks of Printed circuit board engineers. Just like the Auto industry, the Software industry has grown from a few visionaries operating out of their garage with prototypes. Steve Jobs and Bill Gates were the Henry Ford and Louis Chevrolet of their times, who capitalized on ideas already commonly known before they started in the business. In the case of Software development, this moment is generally agreed to be the publication in the 1980s of the specifications for the IBM Personal Computer published by IBM employee Philip Don Estridge. Today his move would be seen as a type of crowd-sourcing.

Until that time, software was *bundled* with the hardware by Original equipment manufacturers (OEMs) such as Data General, Digital Equipment and IBM. When a customer bought a minicomputer, at that time the smallest computer on the market, the computer did not come with Pre-installed software, but needed to be installed by engineers employed by the OEM. Computer hardware companies not only bundled their software, they also placed demands on the location of the hardware in a refrigerated space called a computer room. Most companies had their software on the books for 0 dollars, unable to claim it as an asset (this is similar to financing of popular music in those days). When Data General introduced the Data General Nova, a company called Digidyne wanted to use its RDOS operating system on its own hardware clone. Data General refused to license their software (which was hard to do, since it was on the books as a free asset), and claimed their "bundling rights". The Supreme Court set a precedent called Digidyne v. Data General in 1985. The Supreme Court let a 9th circuit decision stand, and Data General was eventually forced into licensing the Operating System software because it was ruled that restricting the license to only DG hardware was an illegal *tying arrangement*.[5] Soon after, IBM 'published' its DOS source for free, and Microsoft was born. Unable to sustain the loss from lawyer's fees, Data General ended up being taken over by EMC Corporation. The Supreme Court decision made it possible to value software, and also purchase Software patents. The move by IBM was almost a protest at the time. Few in the industry believed that anyone would profit from it other than IBM (through free publicity). Microsoft and Apple were able to thus cash in on 'soft' products. It is hard to imagine today that people once felt that software was worthless without a machine. There are many successful companies today that sell only software products, though there are still many common software licensing problems due to the complexity of designs and poor documentation, leading to patent trolls.

With open software specifications and the possibility of software licensing, new opportunities arose for software tools that then became the de facto standard, such as DOS for operating systems, but also various proprietary word processing and spreadsheet programs. In a similar growth pattern, proprietary development methods became standard Software development methodology.

Types of software

Software includes all the various forms and roles that digitally stored *data* may have and play in a computer (or similar system), regardless of whether the data is used as *code* for a CPU, or other interpreter, or whether it represents other kinds of information. Software thus encompasses a wide array of products that may be developed using different techniques such as ordinary programming languages, scripting languages, microcode, or an FPGA configuration.

The types of software include web pages developed in languages and frameworks like HTML, PHP, Perl, JSP, ASP.NET, XML, and desktop applications like OpenOffice.org, Microsoft Word developed in languages like C, C++, Objective-C, Java, C#, or Smalltalk. Application software usually runs on an underlying software operating systems such as Linux or Microsoft Windows. Software (or firmware) is also used in video games and for the configurable parts of the logic systems of automobiles, televisions, and other consumer electronics.

Practical computer systems divide software systems into three major classes: system software, programming software and application software, although the distinction is arbitrary, and often blurred.

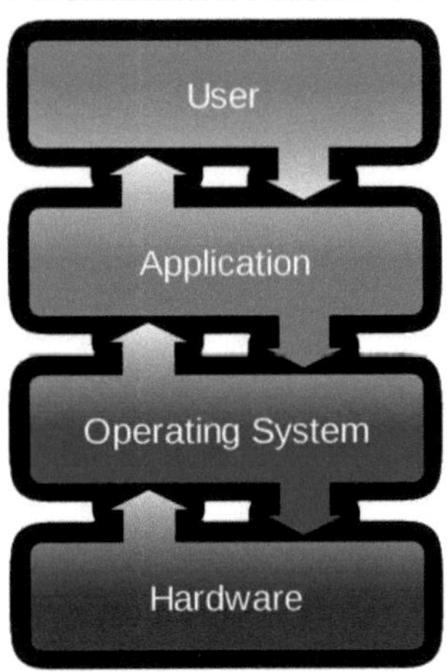

A layer structure showing where the operating system software and application software are situated while running on a typical desktop computer

System software

System software is computer software designed to operate the computer hardware to provide basic functionality and to provide a platform for running application software.[6] [7] System software includes device drivers, operating systems, servers, utilities, and window systems.

System software is responsible for managing a variety of independent hardware components, so that they can work together harmoniously. Its purpose is to unburden the application software programmer from the often complex details of the particular computer being used, including such accessories as communications devices, printers, device readers, displays and keyboards, and also to partition the computer's resources such as memory and processor time in a safe and stable manner.

Programming software

Programming software include tools in the form of programs or applications that software developers use to create, debug, maintain, or otherwise support other programs and applications. The term usually refers to relatively simple programs such as compilers, debuggers, interpreters, linkers, and text editors, that can be combined together to accomplish a task, much as one might use multiple hand tools to fix a physical object. Programming tools are intended to assist a programmer in writing computer programs, and they may be combined in an integrated development environment (IDE) to more easily manage all of these functions.

Application software

Application software is developed to perform in any task that benefits from computation. It is a set of programs that allows the computer to perform a specific data processing job for the user. It is a broad category, and encompasses software of many kinds, including the internet browser being used to display this page. This category includes:

- Business software
- Computer-aided design
- Databases
- Decision-making software
- Educational software
- Image editing
- Industrial automation
- Mathematical software
- Medical software
- Molecular modeling software
- Quantum chemistry and solid state physics software
- Simulation software
- Spreadsheets
- Telecommunications (i.e., the Internet and everything that flows on it)
- Video editing software
- Video games
- Word processing

Software topics

Architecture

Users often see things differently than programmers. People who use modern general purpose computers (as opposed to embedded systems, analog computers and supercomputers) usually see three layers of software performing a variety of tasks: platform, application, and user software.

- Platform software: Platform includes the firmware, device drivers, an operating system, and typically a graphical user interface which, in total, allow a user to interact with the computer and its peripherals (associated equipment). Platform software often comes bundled with the computer. On a PC you will usually have the ability to change the platform software.
- Application software: Application software or Applications are what most people think of when they think of software. Typical examples include office suites and video games. Application software is often purchased separately from computer hardware. Sometimes applications are bundled with the computer, but that does not change the fact that they run as independent applications. Applications are usually independent programs from the operating system, though they are often tailored for specific platforms. Most users think of compilers, databases, and other "system software" as applications.
- User-written software: End-user development tailors systems to meet users' specific needs. User software include spreadsheet templates and word processor templates. Even email filters are a kind of user software. Users create this software themselves and often overlook how important it is. Depending on how competently the user-written software has been integrated into default application packages, many users may not be aware of the distinction between the original packages, and what has been added by co-workers.

Documentation

Most software has software documentation so that the end user can understand the program, what it does, and how to use it. Without clear documentation, software can be hard to use—especially if it is very specialized and relatively complex like Photoshop or AutoCAD.

Developer documentation may also exist, either with the code as comments and/or as separate files, detailing how the programs works and can be modified.

Library

An executable is almost always not sufficiently complete for direct execution. Software libraries include collections of functions and functionality that may be embedded in other applications. Operating systems include many standard Software libraries, and applications are often distributed with their own libraries.

Standard

Since software can be designed using many different programming languages and in many different operating systems and operating environments, software standard is needed so that different software can understand and exchange information between each other. For instance, an email sent from a Microsoft Outlook should be readable from Yahoo! Mail and vice versa.

Execution

Computer software has to be "loaded" into the computer's storage (such as the hard drive or memory). Once the software has loaded, the computer is able to *execute* the software. This involves passing instructions from the application software, through the system software, to the hardware which ultimately receives the instruction as machine code. Each instruction causes the computer to carry out an operation – moving data, carrying out a computation, or altering the control flow of instructions.

Data movement is typically from one place in memory to another. Sometimes it involves moving data between memory and registers which enable high-speed data access in the CPU. Moving data, especially large amounts of it, can be costly. So, this is sometimes avoided by using "pointers" to data instead. Computations include simple operations such as incrementing the value of a variable data element. More complex computations may involve many operations and data elements together.

Quality and reliability

Software quality is very important, especially for commercial and system software like Microsoft Office, Microsoft Windows and Linux. If software is faulty (buggy), it can delete a person's work, crash the computer and do other unexpected things. Faults and errors are called "bugs." Many bugs are discovered and eliminated (debugged) through software testing. However, software testing rarely – if ever – eliminates every bug; some programmers say that "every program has at least one more bug" (Lubarsky's Law). All major software companies, such as Microsoft, Novell and Sun Microsystems, have their own software testing departments with the specific goal of just testing. Software can be tested through unit testing, regression testing and other methods, which are done manually, or most commonly, automatically, since the amount of code to be tested can be quite large. For instance, NASA has extremely rigorous software testing procedures for many operating systems and communication functions. Many NASA based operations interact and identify each other through command programs called software. This enables many people who work at NASA to check and evaluate functional systems overall. Programs containing command software enable hardware engineering and system operations to function much easier together.

License

The software's license gives the user the right to use the software in the licensed environment. Some software comes with the license when purchased off the shelf, or an OEM license when bundled with hardware. Other software comes with a free software license, granting the recipient the rights to modify and redistribute the software. Software can also be in the form of freeware or shareware.

Patents

Software can be patented in some but not all countries; however, software patents can be controversial in the software industry with many people holding different views about it. The controversy over software patents is about specific algorithms or techniques that the software contains, which may not be duplicated by others and considered intellectual property and copyright infringement depending on the severity.

Design and implementation

Design and implementation of software varies depending on the complexity of the software. For instance, design and creation of Microsoft Word software will take much more time than designing and developing Microsoft Notepad because of the difference in functionalities in each one.

Software is usually designed and created (coded/written/programmed) in integrated development environments (IDE) like Eclipse, Emacs and Microsoft Visual Studio that can simplify the process and compile the program. As noted in different section, software is usually created on top of existing software and the application programming interface (API) that the underlying software provides like GTK+, JavaBeans or Swing. Libraries (APIs) are categorized for different purposes. For instance, JavaBeans library is used for designing enterprise applications, Windows Forms library is used for designing graphical user interface (GUI) applications like Microsoft Word, and Windows Communication Foundation is used for designing web services. Underlying computer programming concepts like quicksort, hashtable, array, and binary tree can be useful to creating software. When a program is designed, it relies on the API. For instance, if a user is designing a Microsoft Windows desktop application, he/she might use the .NET Windows Forms library to design the desktop application and call its APIs like *Form1.Close()* and *Form1.Show()*[8] to close or open the application and write the additional operations him/herself that it need to have. Without these APIs, the programmer needs to write these APIs him/herself. Companies like Sun Microsystems, Novell, and Microsoft provide their own APIs so that many applications are written using their software libraries that usually have numerous APIs in them.

Computer software has special economic characteristics that make its design, creation, and distribution different from most other economic goods.[9] [10]

A person who creates software is called a programmer, software engineer, software developer, or code monkey, terms that all have a similar meaning.

Industry and organizations

A great variety of software companies and programmers in the world comprise a software industry. Software can be quite a profitable industry: Bill Gates, the founder of Microsoft was the richest person in the world in 2009 largely by selling the Microsoft Windows and Microsoft Office software products. The same goes for Larry Ellison, largely through his Oracle database software. Through time the software industry has become increasingly specialized.

Non-profit software organizations include the Free Software Foundation, GNU Project and Mozilla Foundation. Software standard organizations like the W3C, IETF develop software standards so that most software can interoperate through standards such as XML, HTML, HTTP or FTP.

Other well-known large software companies include Novell, SAP, Symantec, Adobe Systems, and Corel, while small companies often provide innovation.

See also

- List of software
- Personal computer hardware

References

[1] "Wordreference.com: WordNet 2.0" (http://www.wordreference.com/definition/software). Princeton University, Princeton, NJ. . Retrieved 2007-08-19.

[2] "software..(n.d.)." (http://dictionary.reference.com/browse/software). *Dictionary.com Unabridged (v 1.1)*. . Retrieved 2007-04-13.

[3] Hally, Mike (2005). *Electronic brains/Stories from the dawn of the computer age*. London: British Broadcasting Corporation and Granta Books. p. 79. ISBN 1-86207-663-4.

[4] "John Tukey, 85, Statistician; Coined the Word 'Software'" (http://query.nytimes.com/gst/fullpage. html?res=9500E4DA173DF93BA15754C0A9669C8B63&scp=1&sq=&pagewanted=1). *Obituaries* (New York Times). July 28, 2000. .

[5] "Tying Arrangements and the Computer Industry: Digidyne Corp. vs. Data General". JSTOR 1372482.

[6] http://depts.alverno.edu/cil/mod1/software/system.html

[7] http://searchsoa.techtarget.com/sDefinition/0,,sid26_gci213024,00.html

[8] "MSDN Library" (http://msdn.microsoft.com/en-us/library/default.aspx). . Retrieved 2010-06-14.

[9] v. Engelhardt, Sebastian (2008). "The Economic Properties of Software" (http://ideas.repec.org/p/jrp/jrpwrp/2008-045.html). *Jena Economic Research Papers* 2 (2008–045.). .

[10] Kaminsky, Dan (1999). "Why Open Source Is The Optimum Economic Paradigm for Software" (http://dankaminsky.com/1999/03/02/69/). .

External links

- Software Wikia

Federal_Aviation_Administration

Federal Aviation Administration	
Seal of the Federal Aviation Administration	
Agency overview	
Formed	August 23, 1958
Preceding agency	Civil Aeronautics Administration
Jurisdiction	United States Government
Annual budget	15.956 billion USD (FY2010)
Agency executive	Michael Huerta (Acting), Administrator
Parent agency	United States Department of Transportation
Website	
Official website [1]	
Footnotes	
[2] [3]	

The **Federal Aviation Administration (FAA)** is the national aviation authority of the United States. An agency of the United States Department of Transportation, it has authority to regulate and oversee all aspects of civil aviation in the U.S. The Federal Aviation Act of 1958 created the organization under the name "Federal Aviation Agency", and adopted its current name in 1966 when it became a part of the United States Department of Transportation.

The FAA's major roles include:

- Regulating U.S. commercial space transportation
- Regulating air navigation facilities' geometry and flight inspection standards
- Encouraging and developing civil aeronautics, including new aviation technology
- Issuing, suspending, or revoking pilot certificates
- Regulating civil aviation to promote safety, especially through local offices called Flight Standards District Offices
- Developing and operating a system of air traffic control and navigation for both civil and military aircraft
- Researching and developing the National Airspace System and civil aeronautics
- Developing and carrying out programs to control aircraft noise and other environmental effects of civil aviation

Activities

In December 2000, an organization within FAA called the Air Traffic Organization,[4] or ATO, was set up by presidential executive order. This became the Air Navigation Service Provider for the airspace of the United States and for the New York (Atlantic) and Oakland (Pacific) oceanic areas. It is a full member of the Civil Air Navigation Services Organisation.

FAA issues a number of awards to holders of its licenses. Among these are demonstrated proficiencies as an aviation mechanic, a flight instructor, a 50-year aviator, or as a safe pilot. The latter, the FAA "Wings Program", provides a series of ten badges for pilots who have undergone several hours of training since their last award. A higher level can be claimed each year. For more information see "FAA Advisory Circular 61-91H".

On March 18, 2008, FAA ordered its inspectors to reconfirm that airlines are complying with federal rules after revelations that Southwest Airlines flew dozens of aircraft without certain mandatory inspections.[5] FAA exercises surprise Red Team drills on national airports annually.

Regions and Aeronautical Center Operations

From an operational standpoint, FAA is divided into nine regions plus Headquarters[6] in Washington, DC, the William J. Hughes Technical Center in Atlantic City, and the Mike Monroney Aeronautical Center[7] in Oklahoma City. The nine regions are[8]

- Alaskan[9] – Anchorage, Alaska
- Northwest Mountain[10] – Renton, WA
- Western Pacific[11] – Hawthorne, CA
- Southwest[12] – Fort Worth, TX
- Central[13] – Kansas City, MO
- Great Lakes[14] – Chicago, IL
- Southern[15] – Atlanta, GA
- Eastern[16] – New York City
- New England[17] – Burlington, MA

History

The Air Commerce Act of May 20, 1926, is the cornerstone of the federal government's regulation of civil aviation. This landmark legislation was passed at the urging of the aviation industry, whose leaders believed the airplane could not reach its full commercial potential without federal action to improve and maintain safety standards. The Act charged the Secretary of Commerce with fostering air commerce, issuing and enforcing air traffic rules, licensing pilots, certifying aircraft, establishing airways, and operating and maintaining aids to air navigation. The newly created Aeronautics Branch, operating under the Department of Commerce assumed primary responsibility for aviation oversight.

FAA Headquarters, Washington, D.C.

In fulfilling its civil aviation responsibilities, the Department of Commerce initially concentrated on such functions as safety regulations and the certification of pilots and aircraft. It took over the building and operation of the nation's system of lighted airways, a task that had been begun by the Post Office Department. The Department of Commerce improved aeronautical radio communications and introduced radio beacons as an effective aid to air navigation.

The Aeronautics Branch was renamed the Bureau of Air Commerce in 1934 to reflect its enhanced status within the Department. As commercial flying increased, the Bureau encouraged a group of airlines to establish the first three centers for providing air traffic control (ATC) along the airways. In 1936, the Bureau itself took over the centers and began to expand the ATC system. The pioneer air traffic controllers used maps, blackboards, and mental calculations to ensure the safe separation of aircraft traveling along designated routes between cities.

In 1938, the Civil Aeronautics Act transferred the federal civil aviation responsibilities from the Commerce Department to a new independent agency, the Civil Aeronautics Authority. The legislation also expanded the government's role by giving them the authority and the power to regulate airline fares and to determine the routes that air carriers would serve.

President Franklin D. Roosevelt split the authority into two agencies in 1940, the Civil Aeronautics Administration (CAA) and the Civil Aeronautics Board (CAB). CAA was responsible for ATC, airman and aircraft certification, safety enforcement, and airway development. CAB was entrusted with safety regulation, accident investigation, and economic regulation of the airlines. The CAA was part of the Department of Commerce. The CAB was an independent federal agency.

On the eve of America's entry into World War II, CAA began to extend its ATC responsibilities to takeoff and landing operations at airports. This expanded role eventually became permanent after the war. The application of radar to ATC helped controllers in their drive to keep abreast of the postwar boom in commercial air transportation. In 1946, meanwhile, Congress gave CAA the added task of administering the federal-aid airport program, the first peacetime program of financial assistance aimed exclusively at promoting development of the nation's civil airports.

The approaching era of jet travel, and a series of midair collisions (most notable was the 1956 Grand Canyon mid-air collision), prompted passage of the Federal Aviation Act of 1958. This legislation gave the CAA's functions to a new independent body, the Federal Aviation Agency. The act transferred air safety regulation from the CAB to the new FAA, and also gave the FAA sole responsibility for a common civil-military system of air navigation and air traffic control. The FAA's first administrator, Elwood R. Quesada, was a former Air Force general and adviser to President Eisenhower.

The same year witnessed the birth of the National Aeronautics and Space Administration (NASA), created in the wake of the Soviet launching of the first artificial satellite. NASA assumed NACA's role of aeronautical research while achieving world leadership in space technology and exploration.

In 1967, a new U.S. Department of Transportation (DOT) combined major federal responsibilities for air and surface transport. The Federal Aviation Agency's name changed to the Federal Aviation Administration as it became one of several agencies (e.g., Federal Highway Administration, Federal Railroad Administration, the Coast Guard, and the Saint Lawrence Seaway Commission) within DOT (albeit the largest). The FAA administrator would no longer report directly to the president but would instead report to the Secretary of Transportation. New programs and budget requests would have to be approved by DOT, which would then include these requests in the overall budget and submit it to the president.

At the same time, a new National Transportation Safety Board took over the Civil Aeronautics Board's (CAB) role of investigating and determining the causes of transportation accidents and making recommendations to the secretary of transportation. CAB was merged into DOT with its responsibilities limited to the regulation of commercial airline routes and fares.

FAA gradually assumed additional functions. The hijacking epidemic of the 1960s had already brought the agency into the field of civil aviation security. In response to the hijackings on September 11, 2001, this responsibility is now primarily taken by the Department of Homeland Security. FAA became more involved with the environmental aspects of aviation in 1968 when it received the power to set aircraft noise standards. Legislation in 1970 gave the agency management of a new airport aid program and certain added responsibilities for airport safety. During the 1960s and 1970s, FAA also started to regulate high altitude (over 500 feet) kite and balloon flying.

By the mid-1970s, the agency had achieved a semi-automated air traffic control system using both radar and computer technology. This system required enhancement to keep pace with air traffic growth, however, especially after the Airline Deregulation Act of 1978 phased out the CAB's economic regulation of the airlines. A nationwide strike by the air traffic controllers union in 1981 forced temporary flight restrictions but failed to shut down the airspace system. During the following year, the agency unveiled a new plan for further automating its air traffic control facilities, but progress proved disappointing. In 1994, FAA shifted to a more step-by-step approach that has provided controllers with advanced equipment.[18]

FAA Joint Surveillance Site radar, Canton, Michigan

In 1979 the Congress authorized FAA to work with major commercial airports to define noise pollution contours and investigate the feasibility of noise mitigation by residential retrofit programs. Throughout the 1980s these charters were implemented.

In the 1990s, satellite technology received increased emphasis in FAA's development programs as a means to improvements in communications, navigation, and airspace management. In 1995, the agency assumed responsibility for safety oversight of commercial space transportation, a function begun eleven years before by an office within DOT headquarters. The agency was responsible for the decision to ground flights after the September 11 attacks.

Criticism

Many experts on FAA have been critical of what they perceive as fundamental problems with the agency in conducting oversight on the airlines and pilots, predicated on the belief, as expressed by FAA itself, that both the airlines and pilots are their customers. Retired NASA Office of Inspector General Senior Special Agent Joseph Gutheinz, who formerly was a Special Agent with both the U.S. Department of Transportation Office of Inspector General and FAA Security, is one of the most outspoken critics of FAA. Rather than commend the agency for imposing a 10.2 million dollar fine against Southwest Airlines for its failure to conduct mandatory inspections in 2008, he was quoted as saying the following in an Associated Press story: "Penalties against airlines that violate FAA directives should be stiffer. At $25,000 per violation, (which is how the 10.2 million dollar figure was reached) Gutheinz said, airlines can justify rolling the dice and taking the chance on getting caught. He also said the FAA is often too quick to bend to pressure from airlines and pilots."[19] [20] [21]

Other experts have been critical of the constraints and expectations of the under which the FAA is expected to operate. The dual role of encouraging aerospace travel and regulating aerospace travel are counter intuitive. For example; to levy a heavy penalty upon an airline for violating an FAA regulation which would impact their ability to continue operating would not be considered, encouraging aerospace travel. Risk and safety management author Davic Soucie[22] who served 17 years as a safety inspector for the Federal Aviation Administration including 4 years in the FAA headquarters office in Washington DC discusses this issue in his book *Why Planes Crash - An Accident Investigator's Fight for Safe Skies.*[23]

List of FAA Administrators

- Elwood Richard Quesada (Nov 1, 1958 – Jan 20, 1961)
- Najeeb Halaby (Mar 3, 1961 – Jul 1, 1965)
- William F. McKee (Jul 1, 1965 – Jul 31, 1968)
- John H. Shaffer (Mar 24, 1969 – Mar 14, 1973)
- Alexander Butterfield (Mar 14, 1973 – Mar 31, 1975)
- John L. McLucas (Nov 24, 1975 – Apr 1, 1977)
- Langhorne Bond (May 4, 1977 – Jan 20, 1981)
- J. Lynn Helms (Apr 22, 1981 – Jan 31, 1984)
- Donald D. Engen (Apr 10, 1984 – Jul 2, 1987)
- T. Allan McArtor (Jul 22, 1987 – Feb 17, 1989)
- James B. Busey (Jun 30, 1989 – Dec 4, 1991)
- Thomas C. Richards (Jun 27, 1992 – Jan 20, 1993)
- David R. Hinson (Aug 10, 1993 – Nov 9, 1996)
- Jane Garvey (Aug 4, 1997 – Aug 2, 2002)
- Marion Blakey (Sept 12, 2002 – Sept 13, 2007)
- Robert A. Sturgell (Sept 14, 2007 – Jan 15, 2009)
- Lynne Osmus (Jan 16, 2009 – May 31, 2009)
- Randy Babbitt (Jun 1, 2009 – Dec 6, 2011)

FAA process

Designated Engineering Representative

A Designated Engineering Representative (DER) is an engineer who is appointed to act on behalf of a Company or as an individual Consultant.[24]

- Company DERs act on behalf of their employer and may only approve, or recommend approval, of technical data to the FAA for this company.
- Consultant DERs are appointed to act as an independent DER to approve or recommend approval of technical data to the FAA.

See also

- Air safety
- Airline complaints
- Airway Operational Support
- Civil Aviation Authority
- Commercial Aviation Alternative Fuels Initiative
- Private pilot

References

[1] http://www.faa.gov/

[2] F.A.A. Chief to Lead Industry Group—New York Times (http://www.nytimes.com/2007/08/22/washington/
      22brfs-FAACHIEFTOLE_BRF.html?ex=1189915200&en=6573fa34d3f186ea&ei=5070).

[3] FAA Chief To Become Aerospace Lobbyist—washingtonpost.com (http://www.washingtonpost.com/wp-dyn/content/article/2007/08/
      21/AR2007082101889.html).

[4] Air Traffic Organization (http://ato.faa.gov) Official website.

[5] FAA looking to see if airlines made safety repairs (http://edition.cnn.com/2008/US/03/18/air.safety/index.html).

[6] "FAA.gov" (http://www.faa.gov/about/office_org/headquarters_offices/arc/ro_center/index.cfm?file_name=contact_us_headquarters).
      FAA.gov. 2011-04-06. . Retrieved 2012-03-24.

[7] "FAA.gov" (http://www.faa.gov/about/office_org/headquarters_offices/arc/ro_center/index.
      cfm?file_name=contact_us_aeronautical_center). FAA.gov. 2011-04-06. . Retrieved 2012-03-24.

[8] "FAA.gov" (http://www.faa.gov/about/office_org/headquarters_offices/arc/). FAA.gov. 2012-01-19. . Retrieved 2012-03-24.

[9] "FAA.gov" (http://www.faa.gov/about/office_org/headquarters_offices/arc/ro_center/index.cfm?file_name=contact_us_alaska).
      FAA.gov. 2011-04-06. . Retrieved 2012-03-24.

[10] "FAA.gov" (http://www.faa.gov/about/office_org/headquarters_offices/arc/ro_center/index.
       cfm?file_name=contact_us_northwest_mountain). FAA.gov. 2011-04-06. . Retrieved 2012-03-24.

[11] "FAA.gov" (http://www.faa.gov/about/office_org/headquarters_offices/arc/ro_center/index.
       cfm?file_name=contact_us_western_pacific). FAA.gov. 2011-04-06. . Retrieved 2012-03-24.

[12] "FAA.gov" (http://www.faa.gov/about/office_org/headquarters_offices/arc/ro_center/index.cfm?file_name=contact_us_southwest).
       FAA.gov. 2011-04-06. . Retrieved 2012-03-24.

[13] "FAA.gov" (http://www.faa.gov/about/office_org/headquarters_offices/arc/ro_center/index.cfm?file_name=contact_us_central).
       FAA.gov. 2011-04-06. . Retrieved 2012-03-24.

[14] "FAA.gov" (http://www.faa.gov/about/office_org/headquarters_offices/arc/ro_center/index.cfm?file_name=contact_us_great_lakes).
       FAA.gov. 2011-04-06. . Retrieved 2012-03-24.

[15] "FAA.gov" (http://www.faa.gov/about/office_org/headquarters_offices/arc/ro_center/index.cfm?file_name=contact_us_southern).
       FAA.gov. 2011-04-06. . Retrieved 2012-03-24.

[16] "FAA.gov" (http://www.faa.gov/about/office_org/headquarters_offices/arc/ro_center/index.cfm?file_name=contact_us_eastern).
       FAA.gov. 2011-04-06. . Retrieved 2012-03-24.

[17] "FAA.gov" (http://www.faa.gov/about/office_org/headquarters_offices/arc/ro_center/index.
       cfm?file_name=contact_us_new_england). FAA.gov. 2011-04-06. . Retrieved 2012-03-24.

[18] FAA History (http://www.faa.gov/about/history/brief_history/) from official website.

[19] Southwest Faces Big Penalty on Plane Cracks. (http://www.aviation.com/safety/080307-ap-southwest-faces-penalty.html) Associated
       Press, March 7, 2008.

[20] Military jets rest while go! pilots stay silent. (http://archives.starbulletin.com/2008/03/23/news/story08.html) Associated Press, March
       23, 2008.

[21] Deaths on planes give passengers an up-close view of human frailty (http://www.dailyherald.com/story/?id=144570&src=110).
       Associated Press, February 29, 2008.

[22] whyplanescrash.com (http://www.whyplanescrash.com)

[23] Why Planes Crash - An Accident Investigator's Fight for Safe Skies (http://www.whyplanescrash.com). NYC: Skyhorse Publishing.
       ISBN 161608426X. .

[24] Designated Engineering Representative (DER) (http://www.faa.gov/other_visit/aviation_industry/designees_delegations/
       designee_types/der/).

External links

- FAA (http://www.faa.gov/)
- FAA Safety Briefing (http://www.faa.gov/news/safety_briefing/)
- Pilot Safety Brochures (http://www.faa.gov/pilots/safety/pilotsafetybrochures/)
- ATO News (https://employees.faa.gov/org/linebusiness/ato/)
- FOCUS FAA (https://employees.faa.gov/news/focusfaa/)
- Jane's Airport news on user fees, April 2006 (http://www.janes.com/aerospace/civil/news/jar/
  jar060411_1_n.shtml)

National_Aviation_Facilities_Experimental_Center

The **National Aviation Facilities Experimental Center (NAFEC)** was founded July 1,1958 by the Airways Modernization Board (AMB) near Atlantic City, New Jersey. On November 1, 1959, after passage of the Federal Aviation Act of 1958, it came under the newly created US Federal Aviation Agency (FAA).[1] Its purpose was to conduct research and development on air traffic control computers, transponders, and advanced radar equipment. The success (in terms of funding and research activity) eventually forced the Civil Aeronautics Administration (CAA) to close its own Technical Evaluation and Development Center in Indianapolis starting in 1959.

The computerized air traffic control developed at NAFEC was based on the IBM 9020, special hardware developed by IBM. Software was developed by NAFEC, IBM, and under contract to Computer Usage Company.[2] The system remained in operation until the 1980s.[3] The former 1942 Naval Air Station became the Atlantic City International Airport,[4] and the center is now called the William J. Hughes Technical Center, named for William J. Hughes.[5]

References

[1] "FAA Historical Chronology, 1926–1996" (http://www.faa.gov/about/media/b-chron.pdf). . Retrieved June 2, 2010.

[2] George R. Trimble Jr. (June 24, 2005). "CUC History" (http://corphist.computerhistory.org/corphist/documents/doc-437a4a92bbf21. doc). Computer History Museum. . Retrieved June 2, 2010.

[3] Robert L. Glass (1998). *In the beginning: personal recollections of software pioneers* (http://books.google.com/ books?id=j6NQAAAAMAAJ). IEEE Computer Society. ISBN 9780818679995. .

[4] "Atlantic City Naval Air Station, Egg Harbor Township, New Jersey fact sheet" (http://www.nan.usace.army.mil/project/newjers/factsh/ pdf/atlantic.pdf). US Army Corps of Engineers. December 2007. . Retrieved June 2, 2010.

[5] "William J. Hughes Technical Center" (http://www.faa.gov/about/office_org/headquarters_offices/ato/tc). *Federal Aviation Administration web site*. . Retrieved June 2, 2010.

External links

- "IBM FAA 360/65-9020 display" (http://infolab.stanford.edu/pub/voy/museum/pictures/display/FAA9020. html). *Stanford University Computer History museum*. Retrieved June 2, 2010. pictures of 9020E being recycled

IBM_650

The **IBM 650** (photo [1]) was one of IBM's early computers, and the world's first mass-produced (photo [2]) computer. It was announced in 1953, and over 2000 systems were produced between the first shipment in 1954 and its final manufacture in 1962. Support for the 650 and its component units was withdrawn in 1969.

The 650 is a two-address, bi-quinary coded decimal machine (both data and addresses were decimal), with memory on a rotating drum. The 650 was marketed to scientific and engineering users as well as users of existing IBM unit record equipment (electro-mechanical punched card-processing machines) upgrading from so-called Calculating Punches, like the IBM 604 model, to computers proper.[3] Because of its relatively low cost and simple programming, the 650 pioneered a wide variety of applications, from modeling submarine crew performance[4] to teaching high school students computer programming.

An IBM 650 at Texas A&M University. The IBM 533 card reader and punch is on the right.

Hardware

The basic 650 system consisted of three components:

- Console Unit (IBM 650 [5])
- Power Unit (IBM 655 [6])
- Card Reader/Punch Unit (IBM 533 or IBM 537 [7])

Optional components:

- Disk Unit (IBM 355 [8]) Systems with a disk unit were known as a *IBM RAMAC 650 Data Processing System*
- Card Reader Unit (IBM 543)
- Card Punch Unit (IBM 544)
- Control Unit (IBM 652 [9]) Magnetic Tape Controller
- Auxiliary Unit (IBM 653 [10]) Core storage, index registers, floating point arithmetic
- Auxiliary Alphabetic Unit (IBM 654)
- Magnetic Tape Unit (IBM 727 [11])
- Inquiry Station (IBM 838 [11])

IBM 650 front panel, showing bi-quinary indicators

- Tape To Card Punch IBM 46 Model 3
- Tape To Card Punch IBM 47 Model 3
- Alphabetical Accounting Machine IBM 407

The rotating drum memory (photo [12]) provided 2,000 signed 10-digit words of memory (five characters per word) at addresses 0000 to 1999, which is approximately 8.5 KB in today's units. [13] A Model 4, introduced in 1959, doubled the drum capacity to 4,000 words.[14] A word could not be accessed until its location on the drum surface passed under the read/write heads during rotation (rotating at 12,500 rpm, the non-optimized average access time was 2.5 ms). Because of this timing restriction, the second address in each instruction word was the address of the next instruction. Programs could be optimized by placing instructions around the drum based on the expected execution time of the previous instruction. One specialized instruction, "Table lookup", could high-equal compare a reference 10-digit word with 46 consecutive following words on the drum in one 5ms revolution and then switch to the next track in time for the next 46 words (there were fifty words per track/revolution). This feat was about one-third the speed of a one-thousand times faster binary machine in 1963 (1500 microseconds on the IBM 7040 to 5000 microseconds on the IBM 650 for looking up 46 entries as long as both were programmed in assembler. One higher-level language made the IBM 7040 dramatically slower at table-look-up.

The optional Auxiliary Unit (IBM 653), was introduced on May 3, 1955, providing up to three features:

IBM 650 front panel, rear view

The first IBM 650 in Norway (1959), known as "EMMA". CPU (right), Input-output-unit (middle) and punched card sorter (left). Now at Norwegian Museum of Science and Technology in Oslo.

- Sixty 10-digit words of magnetic core memory at addresses 9000 to 9059; a small *fast memory* (this device gave a memory access time of 96μs, a 26-fold raw improvement relative to the rotating drum), needed for a tape and disk I/O buffer
- Three four-digit index registers at addresses 8005 to 8007; drum addresses were indexed by adding 2000, 4000 or 6000 to them, core

addresses were indexed by adding 0200, 0400 or 0600 to them. If the system had the 4000 word memory drum then indexing was by adding 4000 to the first address for index register A, adding 4000 to the second address for index register B, and by adding 4000 to each of the two addresses for index register C. (the indexing for 4000-word systems only applied to the first address). The 4000-word systems required transistorized read/write circuitry for the drum memory and were available before 1963.

- Floating point – arithmetic instructions with am eight-digit mantissa and two-digit characteristic (offset exponent) – **MMMMMMMMCC**, providing a range of ±0.00000001E-50 to ±0.99999999E+49

The IBM 533 reader punch unit could only read a maximum of 26 columns of alphanumerics from cards in mostly fixed columns. An expansion allowed more but certainly not over 50, as only ten words could be read from a card (five characters per word).

The IBM 650 (pictured here) at the *Haus zur Geschichte der IBM Datenverarbeitung* (House for the History of IBM Data Processing), Sindelfingen, is still running (as of May 2004) and will process an income tax program of the time, with input and output on punched cards.

The IBM 7070, announced 1960, was designed to provide a "transistorized IBM 650" upgrade path. The IBM 1620, introduced in 1959, addressed the lower end of the market. Both were decimal machines, but neither were instruction set compatible.

Vacuum tube circuit module of type used in the 650.

Instruction set

IBM 650 instructions consisted of a two-digit op code, a four-digit data address and the four-digit address of the next instruction. The sign was ignored. The 650 had a 20-digit *accumulator,* divided into 10-digit upper and lower sections with a common sign. Data read from the drum went through a 10-digit *distributer.* Instructions went to a *program register.* Arithmetic was performed by a one-digit adder. Additional instructions were provided for options, such as floating point, core storage, index registers and additional I/O devices. The base machine had 42 op codes. With all options installed, there were 97 op codes.[15]

A classroom in 1960 at the Bronx High School of Science with IBM 650 instruction chart above blackboard, upper right

70	RD	Read
71	PCH	Punch
69	LD	Load distributor
24	STD	Store distributor
10	AU	Add to upper
15	AL	Add to lower
11	SU	Subtract from upper
16	SL	Subtract from lower
60	RAU	Reset (entire accumulator) and add into upper
65	RAL	Reset and add into lower
61	RSU	Reset and subtract into upper
66	RSL	Reset and subtract into lower
20	STL	Store lower into memory
21	STU	Store upper into memory *
22	STDA	Store lower data address
23	STIA	Store lower instruction address
17	AABL	Add absolute to lower
67	RAABL	Reset and add absolute to lower
18	SABL	Subtract absolute from lower
68	RSABL	Reset and subtract absolute into lower
19	MULT	Multiply
14	DIV	Divide
64	DIVRU	Divide and reset upper
44	BRNZU	Branch on non-zero in upper
45	BRNZ	Branch on (accumulator) non-zero
46	BRMIN	Branch on minus
47	BROV	Branch on overflow
90-99	BRD	Branch on 8 in distributor positions 1-10 **
30	SRT	Shift (accumulator) right
31	SRD	Shift and round
35	SLT	Shift left
36	SCT	Shift left and count ***
84	TLU	Table lookup
00	No-Op	No operation
01	Stop	Stop if console switch is set to stop, otherwise no-op

Notes:

- * Value stored takes sign of accumulator, except after a divide operation; then sign of remainder is stored.
- ** Used to allow 533 control panel to signal CPU.
- *** Counts high-order zeros in upper accumulator

Software

Software included:

- BLIS [16] (Bell Laboratories Interpretive System),[17] which used a numeric-only three-address approach
- IPL [18] the first list processing language. The best known version was IPL-V.
- SPACE [19] (Simplified Programming Anyone Can Enjoy) which was a business-oriented two-step compiler (through SOAP)
- Perlis, A.J.; et al. (4/18/58) (PDF). *Internal Translator; IT, A Compiler for the 650* [20]. 650 Library Program 2.1.001.
- Symbolic Optimal Assembly Program, IBM (1957) (PDF). *SOAP II for the IBM 650* [21]. C24-4000-0.
- IBM (1959) (PDF). *FOR TRANSIT Automatic Coding System for the IBM 650* [22]. 28-4028. A version of Fortran which compiled to IT which in turn was compiled to SOAP.
- IBM (1960) (PDF). *FORTRAN Automatic Coding System for the IBM 650* [23]. 29-4047.
- GATE, a simple compiler with one character variable names
- Revised Unified New Compiler IT Basic Language Extended (RUNCIBLE)
- Technical Assembly System (TASS), a macro assembler.

See also

- List of IBM products

References

- IBM (1955) (PDF). *IBM 650 magnetic drum data-processing machine manual of operation.* [24]. 22-6060.
- IBM (1955) (PDF). *IBM Presents the 650 Magnetic Drum Data Processing Machine* [25]. 32-6770.*
- Andree, Richard V. (1958). *Programming the IBM 650 magnetic drum computer and data-processing machine.*
- Knuth, Donald E. (January–March 1986). "The IBM 650: An Appreciation from the Field". *IEEE Annals of the History of Computing* 8 (1): 50–55. doi:10.1109/MAHC.1986.10010. Donald Knuth also dedicated his series of books, *The Art of Computer Programming*, to an IBM 650 computer, with the words "This series of books is affectionately dedicated / to the Type 650 computer once installed at / Case Institute of Technology, / in remembrance of many pleasant evenings."
- IBM 650 Magnetic Drum Data Processing Machine [26]

Notes

[1] http://www-03.ibm.com/ibm/history/exhibits/650/650_ph06.html

[2] http://www-03.ibm.com/ibm/history/exhibits/650/650_ph05.html

[3] 650 Customers (http://www.ibm.com/ibm/history/exhibits/650/650_cu1.html)

[4] Integrated models of cognition systems By Wayne D. Gray, p.36

[5] http://www-03.ibm.com/ibm/history/exhibits/650/650_ph01.html

[6] http://www-03.ibm.com/ibm/history/exhibits/650/650_ph15.html

[7] http://www-03.ibm.com/ibm/history/exhibits/650/650_ph14.html

[8] http://www-03.ibm.com/ibm/history/exhibits/650/650_ph07.html

[9] http://www-03.ibm.com/ibm/history/exhibits/650/650_ph12.html

[10] http://www-03.ibm.com/ibm/history/exhibits/650/650_ph11.html

[11] http://www-03.ibm.com/ibm/history/exhibits/650/650_ph16.html

[12] http://www-03.ibm.com/ibm/history/exhibits/650/650_ph09.html

[13] Each word represents a signed 10-digit decimal number. 2^33 is approximately 8.5 billion (10 digits). To account for the signing, double that -- 2^34 ~= 17 billion. So, on a lower bound, each IBM 650 word can hold information equivalent to 34 bits. Now, 2000x34 = 68000 bits of data. That's 8500 bytes (divide by 8.) which translates to 8.5 KB (divide by 1000) or 8.3 KiB (divide by 1024.)

[14] IBM 640 Model 4 announcement (http://www-03.ibm.com/ibm/history/exhibits/650/650_pr4.html)

[15] http://www.bitsavers.org/pdf/ibm/650/24-5003-0_CPU_Extensions.pdf

[16] http://hopl.murdoch.edu.au/showlanguage.prx?exp=7394&language=BLISS

[17] HOPL shows the name as *BLISS*, which is incorrect; the correct form is given in "Flow-Based Programming" - ISBN 0-442-01771-5

[18] http://hopl.murdoch.edu.au/showlanguage.prx?exp=13&language=IPL

[19] http://hopl.murdoch.edu.au/showlanguage.prx?exp=6599&language=SPACE

[20] http://www.bitsavers.org/pdf/ibm/650/CarnegieInternalTranslator.pdf

[21] http://www.bitsavers.org/pdf/ibm/650/24-4000-0_SOAPII.pdf

[22] http://www.bitsavers.org/pdf/ibm/650/28-4028_FOR_TRANSIT.pdf

[23] http://www.bitsavers.org/pdf/ibm/650/29-4047_FORTRAN.pdf

[24] http://www.bitsavers.org/pdf/ibm/650/22-6060-2_650_OperMan.pdf

[25] http://archive.computerhistory.org/resources/text/IBM/IBM.650.1955.102646125.pdf

[26] http://www-03.ibm.com/ibm/history/exhibits/650/650_intro.html

External links

- IBM Archives: Workhorse of Modern Industry: The IBM 650 (http://www-1.ibm.com/ibm/history/exhibits/650/650_intro.html) Includes a chronology, technical specifications, representative customers, and applications the 650 was used for.
- Weik, Martin H. (March 1961). *A Third Survey of Domestic Electronic Digital Computing Systems* (http://ed-thelen.org/comp-hist/BRL61.html#TOC). Ballistic Research Laboratories (BRL). Report No. 1115. Includes about 40 pages of IBM 650 survey detail: customers, applications, specifications, and costs.
- The IBM 650 at Columbia University (http://www.columbia.edu/acis/history/650.html)
- An IBM 650 Simulator written in Python (http://sim650.googlecode.com)
- An IBM 650 Simulator (http://infinitefish.com/650/650.html)
- Sindelfingen (http://www.stuttgart-tourist.de/ENG/city/sindelfingen.htm) Scroll down to *House for the History of the IBM data processing* where the working IBM 650 pictured above is located. See also History Galore at IBM Museum (http://www.theage.com.au/news/Perspectives/History-galore-at-IBM-museum/2005/01/31/1107020294580.html).
- IBM Museum Sindelfingen (http://www.stuttgart-tourist.de/deutsch/regio/museen/ibm.html) (has the working IBM 650 pictured above)

this next link seems to be broken, try it sometime in April 2006: Haus zur Geschichte der IBM Datenverarbeitung (German) (http://www.netmuseum.de/m-ausgabe.asp?strAufrufer=Liste&strId=791)

- IBM 650 documents at Bitsavers.org (http://www.bitsavers.org/pdf/ibm/650/) (PDF files)
- Video clip of IBM 650 and RAMAC in operation (http://www.ed-thelen.org/comp-hist/HzG-VIDEO-Clip650.wmv), alternate version (http://www.ed-thelen.org/comp-hist/HzG-VIDEO-Clip-650-Trommel.wmv)
- An IBM 650 assembler and Byte code interpreter - Written in PERL (http://www.mta.ca/~eruci/source.htm)
- IBM 650 assembler and byte code interpreters (http://www.mta.ca/~amiller/cs3711/cs3711_ibm650.html)

Initial_public_offering

An **initial public offering (IPO)** or **stock market launch**, is the first sale of stock by a company to the public. It can be used by either small or large companies to raise expansion capital and become publicly traded enterprises. Many companies that undertake an IPO also request the assistance of an investment banking firm acting in the capacity of an underwriter to help them correctly assess the value of their shares, that is, the share price (IPO Initial Public Offerings, 2011).

History

In 1602, the Dutch East India Company was the first company in the world to issue stocks and bonds in an initial public offering (Chambers, 2006).

Reasons for listing

When a company lists its securities on a public exchange, the money paid by investors for the newly issued shares goes directly to the company (in contrast to a later trade of shares on the exchange, where the money passes between investors). An IPO, therefore, allows a company to tap a wide pool of investors to provide itself with capital for future growth, repayment of debt or working capital. A company selling common shares is never required to repay the capital to investors.

Once a company is listed, it is able to issue additional common shares via a secondary offering, thereby again providing itself with capital for expansion without incurring any debt. This ability to quickly raise large amounts of capital from the market is a key reason many companies seek to go public.

There are several benefits to being a public company, namely:

- Bolstering and diversifying equity base
- Enabling cheaper access to capital
- Exposure, prestige and public image
- Attracting and retaining better management and employees through liquid equity participation
- Facilitating acquisitions
- Creating multiple financing opportunities: equity, convertible debt, cheaper bank loans, etc.

Disadvantages of an IPO

There are several disadvantages to completing an initial public offering, namely:

- Significant legal, accounting and marketing costs
- Ongoing requirement to disclose financial and business information
- Meaningful time, effort and attention required of senior management
- Risk that required funding will not be raised
- Public dissemination of information which may be useful to competitors, suppliers and customers.

Procedure

IPOs generally involve one or more investment banks known as "underwriters". The company offering its shares, called the "issuer", enters a contract with a lead underwriter to sell its shares to the public. The underwriter then approaches investors with offers to sell these shares.

The sale (allocation and pricing) of shares in an IPO may take several forms. Common methods include:

- Best efforts contract
- Firm commitment contract
- All-or-none contract
- Bought deal
- Dutch auction

A large IPO is usually underwritten by a "syndicate" of investment banks led by one or more major investment banks (lead underwriter). Upon selling the shares, the underwriters keep a commission based on a percentage of the value of the shares sold (called the gross spread). Usually, the lead underwriters, i.e. the underwriters selling the largest proportions of the IPO, take the highest commissions—up to 8% in some cases.

Multinational IPOs may have many syndicates to deal with differing legal requirements in both the issuer's domestic market and other regions. For example, an issuer based in the E.U. may be represented by the main selling syndicate in its domestic market, Europe, in addition to separate syndicates or selling groups for US/Canada and for Asia. Usually, the lead underwriter in the main selling group is also the lead bank in the other selling groups.

Because of the wide array of legal requirements and because it is an expensive process, IPOs typically involve one or more law firms with major practices in securities law, such as the Magic Circle firms of London and the white shoe firms of New York City.

Public offerings are sold to both institutional investors and retail clients of underwriters. A licensed securities salesperson (Registered Representative in the USA and Canada) selling shares of a public offering to his clients is paid a commission from their dealer rather than their client. In cases where the salesperson is the client's advisor it is notable that the financial incentives of the advisor and client are not aligned.

In the US sales can only be made through a final prospectus cleared by the Securities and Exchange Commission.

Investment dealers will often initiate research coverage on companies so their Corporate Finance departments and retail divisions can attract and market new issues.

The issuer usually allows the underwriters an option to increase the size of the offering by up to 15% under certain circumstance known as the greenshoe or overallotment option.

Auction

A venture capitalist named Bill Hambrecht has attempted to devise a method that can reduce the inefficient process. He devised a way to issue shares through a Dutch auction as an attempt to minimize the extreme underpricing that underwriters were nurturing. Underwriters, however, have not taken to this strategy very well which is understandable given that auctions are threatening large fees otherwise payable. Though not the first company to use Dutch auction, Google is one established company that went public through the use of auction. Google's share price rose 17% in its first day of trading despite the auction method. Brokers close to the IPO report that the underwriters actively discouraged institutional investors from buying to reduce demand and send the initial price down. The resulting low share price was then used to "illustrate" that auctions generally don't work.

Perception of IPOs can be controversial. For those who view a successful IPO to be one that raises as much money as possible, the IPO was a total failure. For those who view a successful IPO from the kind of investors that eventually gained from the underpricing, the IPO was a complete success. It's important to note that different sets of investors bid in auctions versus the open market—more institutions bid, fewer private individuals bid. Google may be a special case, however, as many individual investors bought the stock based on long-term valuation shortly after it launched its IPO, driving it beyond institutional valuation.

Pricing of IPO

The underpricing of initial public offerings (IPO) has been well documented in different markets (Ibbotson, 1975; Ritter 1984; Levis, 1990; McGuinness, 1992; Drucker and Puri, 2007). While issuers always try to maximize their issue proceeds, the underpricing of IPOs has constituted a serious anomaly in the literature of financial economics. Many financial economists have developed different models to explain the underpricing of IPOs. Some of the models explained it as a consequence of deliberate underpricing by issuers or their agents. In general, smaller issues are observed to be underpriced more than large ones (Ritter, 1984; Ritter, 1991; Levis, 1990).

Historically, some of IPOs both globally and in the United States have been underpriced. The effect of "initial underpricing" an IPO is to generate additional interest in the stock when it first becomes publicly traded. Through flipping, this can lead to significant gains for investors who have been allocated shares of the IPO at the offering price. However, underpricing an IPO results in "money left on the table"—lost capital that could have been raised for the company had the stock been offered at a higher price. One great example of all these factors at play was seen with theglobe.com IPO which helped fuel the IPO mania of the late 90's internet era. Underwritten by Bear Stearns on November 13, 1998, the stock had been priced at $9 per share, and famously jumped 1000% at the opening of trading all the way up to $97, before deflating and closing at $63 after large sell offs from institutions flipping the stock. Although the company did raise about $30 million from the offering it is estimated that with the level of demand for the offering and the volume of trading that took place the company might have left upwards of $200 million on the table.

The danger of overpricing is also an important consideration. If a stock is offered to the public at a higher price than the market will pay, the underwriters may have trouble meeting their commitments to sell shares. Even if they sell all of the issued shares, if the stock falls in value on the first day of trading, it may lose its marketability and hence even more of its value.

Underwriters, therefore, take many factors into consideration when pricing an IPO, and attempt to reach an offering price that is low enough to stimulate interest in the stock, but high enough to raise an adequate amount of capital for the company. The process of determining an optimal price usually involves the underwriters ("syndicate") arranging share purchase commitments from leading institutional investors.

On the other hand, some researchers (e.g. Geoffrey C., and C. Swift, 2009) believe that IPOs are not being under-priced deliberately by issuers and/or underwriters, but the price-rocketing phenomena on issuance days are due to investors' over-reaction (Friesen & Swift, 2009).

Some algorithms to determine underpricing: IPO Underpricing Algorithms

Issue price

A company that is planning an IPO appoints lead managers to help it decide on an appropriate price at which the shares should be issued. There are two ways in which the price of an IPO can be determined: either the company, with the help of its lead managers, fixes a price (fixed price method) or the price is arrived at through the process of book building.

Note: Not all IPOs are eligible for delivery settlement through the DTC system, which would then either require the physical delivery of the stock certificates to the clearing agent bank's custodian, or a delivery versus payment (DVP) arrangement with the selling group brokerage firm.

Quiet period

There are two time windows commonly referred to as "quiet periods" during an IPO's history. The first and the one linked above is the period of time following the filing of the company's S-1 but before SEC staff declare the registration statement effective. During this time, issuers, company insiders, analysts, and other parties are legally restricted in their ability to discuss or promote the upcoming IPO (U.S. Securities and Exchange Commission, 2005).

The other "quiet period" refers to a period of 40 calendar days following an IPO's first day of public trading. During this time, insiders and any underwriters involved in the IPO are restricted from issuing any earnings forecasts or research reports for the company. Regulatory changes enacted by the SEC as part of the Global Settlement enlarged the "quiet period" from 25 days to 40 days on July 9, 2002. When the quiet period is over, generally the underwriters will initiate research coverage on the firm. Additionally, the NASDAQ and NYSE have approved a rule mandating a 10-day quiet period after a Secondary Offering and a 15-day quiet period both before and after expiration of a "lock-up agreement" for a securities offering.

Stag profit

Stag profit is a stock market term used to describe a situation before and immediately after a company's Initial public offering (or any new issue of shares). A **stag** is a party or individual who subscribes to the new issue expecting the price of the stock to rise immediately upon the start of trading. Thus, stag profit is the financial gain accumulated by the party or individual resulting from the value of the shares rising.

For example, one might expect a certain I.T. company to do particularly well and purchase a large volume of their stock or shares before flotation on the stock market. Once the price of the shares has risen to a satisfactory level the person will choose to sell their shares and make a stag profit.

Largest IPOs

1. Agricultural Bank of China $22.1 billion (2010)[1]
2. Industrial and Commercial Bank of China $21.9 billion (2006)[2]
3. American International Assurance $20.5 billion (2010)[3]
4. Visa Inc. $19.7 billion (2008)[4]
5. General Motors $18.1 billion (2010)[5]

Value of IPOs

The US last topped the IPO league tables in 2008; then east overtook west with China (Shanghai, Shenzhen and Hong Kong) raising $73 billion (almost double the amount of money raised on the New York Stock Exchange and Nasdaq combined) up to the end of November 2011. The Hong Kong Stock Exchange raised 30.9 billion in 2011 as the top course for the third year in a row, while New York raised 30.7 billion.[6]

See also

- Alternative public offering
- Direct public offering
- Equity carve-out
- Mergers and acquisitions (M&A)
- Private placement
- Public offering without listing
- Reverse IPO
- Seasoned equity offering

- SEC Form S-1 (Registration form for certain types of issuers)
- Secondary market offering
- Venture capital

References

[1] "Agricultural Bank of China Sets IPO Record as Size Raised to $22.1 Billion" (http://www.bloomberg.com/news/2010-08-15/ agricultural-bank-of-china-sets-ipo-record-with-22-1-billion-boosted-sale.html). *Bloomberg*. 2010-08-15. .

[2] "ICBC completed its record $21.9 billion IPO in October 2006" (http://www.bloomberg.com/news/2010-07-28/ icbc-to-seek-as-much-as-6-6-billion-in-rights-offer-to-replenish-capital.html). *Bloomberg*. 2010-07-28. .

[3] "AIA's IPO Boosted to $20.5 Billion With Overallotment" (http://www.bloomberg.com/news/2010-10-29/ aia-s-ipo-boosted-to-20-5-billion-with-overallotment-update1-.html). *Bloomberg*. 2010-10-29. .

[4] Grocer, Stephen (2010-11-17). "How GM's IPO Stacks Up Against the Biggest IPOs on Record" (http://blogs.wsj.com/deals/2010/11/ 17/how-gms-ipo-stacks-up-against-the-biggest-ipos-on-record/). *Wall Street Journal*. .

[5] "GM Says Total Offering Size $23.1 Billion Including Overallotment Options" (http://www.bloomberg.com/news/2010-11-26/ gm-says-total-offering-size-23-1-billion-including-overallotment-options.html), *Bloomberg*, 2010-11-26,

[6] "China eclipses US as top IPO venue" (http://www.ft.com/intl/cms/s/0/d9733718-2c4a-11e1-b7df-00144feabdc0.html). December 28, 2011. .

Further reading

- Gregoriou, Greg (2006). *Initial Public Offerings (IPOs)* (http://books.elsevier.com/finance/ ?isbn=0750679751). Butterworth-Heineman, an imprint of Elsevier. ISBN 0-7506-7975-1.
- Killian, Linda (2006). *IPOs for Everyone* (http://www.renaissancecapital.com/RenCap/AboutUs/Book.aspx). Wiley. ISBN 978-0-471-39915-5.
- Facebook IPO Largest in Tech World History Facebook Initial Public Offering Largest Tech IPO in History
- Goergen, M.; Khurshed, A.; Mudambi, R. (2007). "The Long-run Performance of UK IPOs: Can it be Predicted?". *Managerial Finance* 33 (6): 401–419. doi:10.1108/03074350710748759.
- Loughran, T.; Ritter, J. R. (2004). "Why Has IPO Underpricing Changed Over Time?" (http://bear.cba.ufl.edu/ ritter/publ_papers/Why has IPO Underpricing Changed Over Time.pdf). *Financial Management* 33 (3): 5–37.
- Loughran, T.; Ritter, J. R. (2002). "Why Don't Issuers Get Upset About Leaving Money on the Table in IPOs?". *Review of Financial Studies* 15 (2): 413–443. doi:10.1093/rfs/15.2.413.
- Khurshed, A.; Mudambi, R. (2002). "The Short Run Price Performance of Investment Trust IPOs on the UK Main Market". *Applied Financial Economics* 12 (10): 697–706. doi:10.1080/09603100010025706.
- Bradley, D. J.; Jordan, B. D.; Ritter, J. R. (2003). "The Quiet Period Goes Out with a Bang". *Journal of Finance* 58 (1): 1–36. doi:10.1111/1540-6261.00517.
- Goergen, M.; Khurshed, A.; Mudambi, R. (2006). "The Strategy of Going Public: How UK Firms Choose Their Listing Contracts". *Journal of Business Finance and Accounting* 33 (1&2): 306–328. SSRN 886408.
- Mudambi, R.; Treichel, M. Z. (2005). "Cash Crisis in Newly Public Internet-based Firms: An Empirical Analysis". *Journal of Business Venturing* 20 (4): 543–571. doi:10.1016/j.jbusvent.2004.03.003.
- Drucker, Steven; Puri, M. (2007). "Banks in Capital Markets". In Eckbo, B. E.. *Handbook of Corporate Finance*. 1. Boston: Elsevier. ISBN 978-0-444-50898-0.
- "IPO Definitions" (http://www.ipoinitialpublicofferings.com/ipo-definitions.htm). IPO Initial Public Offerings. Retrieved 14 September 2011.
- Mondo Visione web site: Chambers, Clem. "Who needs stock exchanges?" (http://www.mondovisione.com/ exchanges/handbook-articles/who-needs-stock-exchanges/) *Exchanges Handbook*. Published 2006-07-14. Accessed 21 September 2011
- Friesen, Geoffrey C.; Swift, Christopher (2009). "Overreaction in the thrift IPO aftermarket". *Journal of Banking & Finance* 33 (7): 1285–1298. doi:10.1016/j.jbankfin.2009.01.002.
- Anderlini, Jamil (August 13, 2010). "AgBank IPO officially the world's biggest" (http://www.ft.com/cms/s/0/ ff7d528c-a6bc-11df-8d1e-00144feabdc0.html?ftcamp=rss). Financial Times. Retrieved 2010-08-13.

- Hu, Bei and Vannucci, Cecile. Bloomberg.com (http://www.bloomberg.com/news/2010-10-28/ aia-will-have-hong-kong-trading-debut-today-after-rising-in-gray-market-.html) Published 2010-10-29. Retrieved 2011-09-21
- "Pricing the 'biggest IPO in history'" (http://www.atimes.com/atimes/China_Business/HI29Cb01.html). Published 2006-09-29. Accessed 2011-09-21
- "Quiet Period" (http://www.sec.gov/answers/quiet.htm). Securities and Exchange Commission. August 18, 2005. Retrieved 2008-03-04. "The federal securities laws do not define the term "quiet period," which is also referred to as the "waiting period." However, historically, a quiet period extended from the time a company files a registration statement with the SEC until SEC staff declared the registration statement "effective." During that period, the federal securities laws limited what information a company and related parties can release to the public."

External links

- Initial Public Offering (IPO) Definition and Calendar, Wikinvest
- How IPO works - HowStuff Works (http://www.howstuffworks.com/ipo1.htm,)

Cuthbert_Hurd

Cuthbert Corwin Hurd (1911–1996) was an American computer scientist and entrepreneur, who was instrumental in helping the International Business Machines Corporation develop its first general-purpose computers.[1]

Life

Hurd was born April 5, 1911 in Estherville, Iowa. He received his B.A. in mathematics from Drake University in 1932, his M.S. in mathematics from Iowa State College in 1934, and his Ph.D. in mathematics from the University of Illinois in 1936. Waldemar Joseph Trjitzinsky was his advisor, and dissertation was *Asymptotic theory of linear differential equations singular in the variable of differentiation and in a parameter*.[2] He did post doctorate work at Columbia University and the Massachusetts Institute of Technology (MIT). He was assistant professor at Michigan State University from 1936 to 1942.[3]

The IBM 650 was developed by the division headed by Cuthbert Hurd

During World War II Hurd taught at the US Coast Guard Academy with the rank of Lieutenant Commander, and co-authored the textbook for teaching Mathematics to mariners. From 1945 to 1947 he was dean of Allegheny College. In 1947 he moved to Oak Ridge, Tennessee, where he worked for Union Carbide as mathematician at the United States Atomic Energy Commission facility Oak Ridge National Laboratory. He taught and later served as a technical research head under Alston Scott Householder. At Oak Ridge he supervised the installation of an IBM 602 calculating punched card machine to automate the tracking of material in the facility, and saw the potential for automating the massive amounts of computation needed for nuclear Physics research. In February 1948 he was invited to the dedication of the IBM Selective Sequence Electronic Calculator (SSEC), a custom-built machine in New York city. He asked if the SSEC could be used for calculations being done at Oak Ridge for the NEPA project to power an airplane with a nuclear reactor, but the demands for the SSEC produced a backlog. In the meanwhile, he requested that the first IBM 604 calculating card punch be delivered to Oak Ridge. It was, but the calculations remained slow with the limited electronics in the 604.[4]

IBM

From 1949 to 1962 he worked at IBM, where he founded the Applied Science Department and pushed reluctant management into the world of computing.[3] Hurd hired John von Neumann as a consultant. The eccentric genius was known for his fast driving, and IBM often would pay von Neumann's traffic fines. They developed a personal friendship, with Hurd visiting von Neumann in Walter Reed Army Medical Center as he was dying of cancer.[5]

At the time, IBM calculators were programmed by plugging and unplugging wires manually into large panels. The concept of storing the program as well as data in computer memory was generally called the Von Neumann architecture (although others developed the concept about the same time). IBM had built the experimental stored-program SSEC, but company president Thomas J. Watson favored basing commercial products on punched card technology with manual programming. Hurd hired a team who would be the first professional computer software writers, such as John Backus and Fred Brooks.[6] The first step was to offer a calculator that could be programmed on punch cards in addition to a manual plugboard. This was the Card-Programmed Electronic Calculator, announced in May 1949. It was essentially a commercialized version of experiments done by Wallace John Eckert and customers at Northrop Corporation, but became a very popular product, shipping several thousand units in various models.[7] [8]

Based on this demand, Hurd advised new company president Tom Watson, Jr. to build the first IBM commercial stored program computer, first called the Defense Calculator. It was marketed as the IBM 701 in 1952.[9] There were 18 model 701 machines built (in addition to the Engineering development machine).

In 1953 Hurd convinced IBM management to develop what became the IBM 650 Magnetic Drum Data Processing Machine. Although the UNIVAC I (and Ferranti Mark 1 in England[10]) had been introduced earlier than any IBM computer, its high price (while IBM offered monthly leases) limited sales. The lower expense of the 650 meant it could be purchased in much larger quantities. Almost 2000 were produced between 1953 and 1962, to commercial customers as well as academics.[11] On January 19, 1955 Hurd became director of the IBM Electronic Data Processing Machines Division when T. Vincent Learson was promoted to Vice President of Sales.[12] In 1955, Hurd made a proposal to Edward Teller for a computer to be used at the Lawrence Livermore Laboratory. This would evolve into the IBM "Stretch" project. The ambitious promises made for the performance of the machine were not met when it was finally delivered in 1961 as the model 7030, although techniques developed and lessons learned in its design were used on other IBM products.[13]

California

After 1962 he served as chairman of the Computer Usage Company, the first independent computer software company, and president from 1970 through 1974.[14]

He then consulted for various firms in Silicon valley, and served as an expert witness in the IBM antritrust cases.[15] From 1978 to 1986, Hurd served as chairman for Picodyne Corporation, which he co-founded with H. Dean Brown. Hurd was a founder of Quintus Computer Systems in 1983 with William Kornfeld, Lawrence Byrd, Fernando Perreira and David H. D. Warren to commercialize a Prolog compiler.[16] Hurd was president and chairman until Quintus was sold to Intergraph Corporation in October 1989.[3] [17]

In 1967 Drake awarded him an honorary LLD degree.[18] In 1986 Cuthbert C. Hurd received the IEEE Computer Pioneer award by the IEEE Computer Society for his contributions to early computing. In his later life he lived in Portola Valley, California, became an avid gardener and studied native California plants. A variety of *Arctostaphylos manzanita* is named Dr. Hurd for him.[19] He died there May 22, 1996. He endowed scholarships in Mathematics and Computer Science at Stanford University.[20]

Publications

- "Asymptotic theory of linear differential equations singular in the variable of differentiation and in a parameter" [21]. *Tohoku Mathematical Journal* **44 (first series)**: pp. 243–274. 1938.
- "Asymptotic theory of linear differential equations containing two parameters" [21]. *Tohoku Mathematical Journal* **45 (first series)**: pp. 58–68. 1939.
- 1943, *Mathematics for Mariners* with Chester E. Dimick. New York: D Van Nostrand Company Inc, 1943.
- 1950, "The IBM Card-Programmed Electronic Calculator" in: *Proceedings, Seminar on Scientific Computation November, 1949*, IBM, p. 37-41.
- 1955, "Mechanical Translation: New Challenge to Communication Ornstein", in: *Science* 21 October 1955: pp. 745–748.
- Nicholas Metropolis, Jack Howlett, Gian-Carlo Rota, ed. (November 1980). "Computer Developments at IBM" [22]. *A history of computing in the twentieth century: a collection of essays*. Academic Press. ISBN 9780124916500.
- 1983. *Special Issue: The IBM 701 Thirtieth Anniversary - IBM Enters the Computing Field*, Annals of the History of Computing, Vol. 5 (No. 2), 1983
- 1985, "A note on early Monte Carlo computations and scientific meetings", in: *IEEE Annals of the History of Computing archive*, Volume 7, Issue 2 (April 1985) pp 141–155.
- 1986, "Prologue," IEEE Annals of the History of Computing, vol. 8, no. 1, pp. 6–7, Jan-Mar, 1986

See also

- History of computing
- Timeline of computing
- History of computing hardware
- IBM 700/7000 series

References

[1] Laurance Zuckerman (June 2, 1996). "Cuthbert Hurd, 85, Computer Pioneer at I.B.M" (http://query.nytimes.com/gst/fullpage. html?res=9F0DE4DE1F39F931A35755C0A960958260). *New York Times*. . Retrieved May 24, 2010.

[2] W. J. Trjitzinsky (1938). "Singular point problems in the theory of linear differential equations" (http://projecteuclid.org/euclid.bams/ 1183500399). *Bulletin of the American Mathematical Society* **44** (4): 209–223. doi:10.1090/S0002-9904-1938-06716-X. .

[3] John A. N. Lee (1995). "Cuthbert C. Hurd" (http://books.google.com/books?id=ocx4Jc12mkgC&pg=PA388). *International biographical dictionary of computer pioneers*. Taylor & Francis for IEEE Computer Society Press. pp. 388–389. ISBN 9781884964473. .

[4] Robert Seidel (November 18, 1994). "An Interview with Cuthbert C. Hurd" (http://purl.umn.edu/107370). Charles Babbage Institute, University of Minnesota. . Retrieved June 3, 2010.

[5] Nancy Stern (January 20, 1981). "An Interview with Cuthbert C. Hurd" (http://purl.umn.edu/107368). Charles Babbage Institute, University of Minnesota. . Retrieved June 3, 2010.

[6] "John Backus" (http://www.ibm.com/ibm/history/exhibits/builders/builders_backus3.html). *IBM Builders reference room*. . Retrieved May 25, 2010.

[7] Frank da Cruz. "The IBM Card Programmed Calculator" (http://www.columbia.edu/acis/history/cpc.html). *Chronology of Computing at Columbia University*. . Retrieved June 3, 2010.

[8] "Card-Programmed Electronic Calculator" (http://www.ibm.com/ibm/history/exhibits/space/space_card.html). *IBM archives*. . Retrieved June 3, 2010.

[9] "701 Team" (http://www.ibm.com/ibm/history/exhibits/701/701_team.html). *IBM archives*. . Retrieved May 25, 2010.

[10] Chris Malcolm (May 4, 2000). "Who Made the First Computer?" (http://www.dai.ed.ac.uk/homes/cam/fcomp.shtml). . Retrieved June 5, 2010.

[11] "Workhorse of modern industry: The IBM 650" (http://www.ibm.com/ibm/history/exhibits/650/650_intro.html). *IBM archives*. . Retrieved May 25, 2010.

[12] Emerson W. Pugh (1995). *Building IBM: shaping an industry and its technology* (http://books.google.com/books?id=Bc8BGhSOawgC& pg=PA364). MIT Press. p. 364. ISBN 9780262161473. .

[13] "Timeline of the IBM Stretch/Harvest Era (1956–1961)" (http://archive.computerhistory.org/resources/text/IBM/Stretch/102636400. txt). Computer History Museum. . Retrieved May 25, 2010.

[14]   Charles R. Fillerup (August 28, 1995). "An Interview with Cuthbert C. Hurd" (http://purl.umn.edu/107371). Charles Babbage Institute,
       University of Minnesota. . Retrieved June 3, 2010.
[15]   "IBM Antitrust Suit Records1950-1982" (http://www.hagley.lib.de.us/library/collections/manuscripts/findingaids/ibmantitrustpart2.
       ACC1980.htm). *finding aid*. Hagley Museum and Library. . Retrieved June 1, 2010.
[16]   *The Artificial intelligence report* (http://books.google.com/books?id=xILpAAAAMAAJ). Artificial Intelligence Publications. 1983. .
[17]   David E. Weisberg (2008). "Intergraph" (http://www.cadhistory.net/chapters/14_Intergraph.pdf). *The Engineering Design
       Revolution:The People, Companies and Computer Systems That Changed Forever the Practice of Engineering*. . Retrieved May 26, 2010.
[18]   "Honorary Degrees Awarded by Drake University" (http://www.drake.edu/president/honorarydegrees.php). *Drake University office of
       the president*. . Retrieved May 25, 2010.
[19]   Saratoga Horticultural Research Foundation (2003). "Manzanita introductions of the Saratoga Horticultural Foundation" (http://www.
       stanford.edu/~rawlings/PDF/003.pdf). . Retrieved May 25, 2010.
[20]   "Endowed Graduate Financial Aid Funds" (http://engineering.stanford.edu/about/AR97-98/funds.html). Stanford School of
       Engineering. 1997. . Retrieved May 26, 2010.
[21]   http://www.math.tohoku.ac.jp/tmj/1stSpTMJpv.pdf
[22]   http://books.google.com/books?id=_H9QAAAAMAAJ

Further reading

- 1954, "Russian is turned into English by a fast electronic translator" (http://www.hutchinsweb.me.uk/sources/
  GU-IBM-NYT-1954-Plumb.pdf.) by Robert K.Plumb in: *New York Times*, 8 January 1954, p. 1 (front
  page),col.5.
- 1996, "Update," in: *Computer*, vol. 29, no. 7, pp. 92–94, Jul., 1996
- Atsushi Akera (Winter 2002). "IBM's Early Adaptation to Cold War Markets: Cuthbert Hurd and His Applied
  Science Field Men". *The Business History Review* **72** (4): 767–802. JSTOR 4127709.

External links

- Cuthbert C. Hurd Papers, 1946-1992 (http://purl.umn.edu/40811) at the Charles Babbage Institute, University
  of Minnesota.
- Three oral history interviews with Cuthbert Hurd, 20 January 1981 (http://purl.umn.edu/107368), 18
  November 1994 (http://purl.umn.edu/107370) and August 28 1995 (http://purl.umn.edu/107371), Charles
  Babbage Institute, University of Minnesota. Hurd discusses International Business Machines research in computer
  technology, IBM's support for academic research on computers, and his own work at IBM—especially on the
  IBM 701, 704 and 705 computers. He also describes John von Neumann and his contributions to the development
  of computer technology. Discusses interactions with Oak Ridge National Laboratory and Los Alamos National
  Laboratory.

IBM_System/360

Designer	IBM
Bits	32-bit
Introduced	1964
Design	CISC
Type	Register-Register Register-Memory Memory-Memory
Encoding	Variable (2, 4 or 6 bytes long)
Branching	Condition code, indexing, counting
Endianness	Big
Page size	N/A, except for 360/67
Open	Yes
Registers	
General purpose	16 32-bit
Floating point	4 64-bit

IBM mainframe	Architecture
700/7000 series	varied
System/360	System/360
System/370	System/370
	S/370-XA
	ESA/370
System/390	ESA/390 (ARCHLVL 1)
zSeries	z/Architecture 1 (ARCHLVL 2)
System z9	
System z10	z/Architecture 2 (ARCHLVL 3)
zEnterprise z196	
zEnterprise z114	

The **IBM System/360 (S/360)** was a mainframe computer system family announced by IBM on April 7, 1964, and delivered between 1965 and 1978[1] . It was the first family of computers designed to cover the complete range of applications, from small to large, both commercial and scientific. The design made a clear distinction between architecture and implementation, allowing IBM to release a suite of compatible designs at different prices. All but the most expensive systems used microcode to implement the instruction set, which featured 8-bit byte addressing and binary, decimal and floating-point calculations.

An IBM System/360 in use at Volkswagen.

The slowest System/360 models announced in 1964 ranged in speed from 0.0018 to 0.034 MIPS;[2] the fastest System/360 models were approximately 50 times as fast[3] with 8 kB and up to 8 MB of internal main memory,[3] though the latter was unusual, and up to 8 megabytes of slower Large Core Storage (LCS). A large system might have as little as 256 kB of main storage, but 512 kB, 768 kB or 1024 kB was more common.

The 360s were extremely successful in the market, allowing customers to purchase a smaller system with the knowledge they would always be able to migrate upward if their needs grew, without reprogramming of application software. The design is considered by many to be one of the most successful computers in history, influencing computer design for years to come.

The chief architect of the S/360 was Gene Amdahl, and the project was managed by Fred Brooks, responsible to Chairman Thomas J. Watson Jr.[3] The 360's commercial release was piloted by another of Watson's lieutenants John R. Opel who managed the launch of IBM's System 360 mainframe family in 1964.[4]

Application level compatibility (with some restrictions) for System/360 software is maintained until present day with the IBM zSeries computers.

System/360 history

A family of computers

Contrasting with at-the-time normal industry practice, IBM created an entire series of computers (or CPUs) from small to large, low to high performance, all using the same instruction set (with two exceptions for specific markets). This feat allowed customers to use a cheaper model and then upgrade to larger systems as their needs increased without the time and expense of rewriting software. IBM was the first manufacturer to exploit microcode technology to implement a compatible range of computers of widely differing performance, although the largest, fastest, models had hard-wired logic instead.

An IBM System/360-20 (w/ front panels removed), with IBM 2560 MFCM (Multi-Function Card Machine)

This flexibility greatly lowered barriers to entry. With other vendors (with the notable exception of ICT), customers had to choose between machines they could outgrow and machines that were potentially overpowered (and thus too expensive). This meant that many companies simply did not buy computers.

Models

IBM initially announced a series of six computers and forty common peripherals. IBM eventually delivered fourteen models, including rare one-off models for NASA. The cheapest model was the S/360-20 with as little as 4 K of core memory, eight 16-bit registers instead of the sixteen 32-bit registers of real 360s, and an instruction set that was a

IBM System/360 Model 30 at the Computer History Museum.

subset of that used by the rest of the range. (The Model 20 was suited for smaller businesses — yet it had the IBM name and salesforce.)

The initial announcement in 1964 included Models 30, 40, 50, 60, 62, and 70. The first three were low- to middle-range systems aimed at the IBM 1400 series market. All three were sold first during mid-1965. The last three, intended to replace the 7000 series machines, were never sold and were replaced by the 65 and 75, which was first delivered during November 1965, and January 1966, respectively.

Later additions to cheaper models included the 20 (1966, mentioned above), 22 (1971), and 25 (1968). The Model 22 was a recycled Model 30 with minor limitations: a smaller maximum memory configuration, and slower I/O channels which limited it to slower and lower-capacity disk and tape devices than on the 30.

The Model 44 (1966) was a variant aimed at the mid-range scientific market with hardware floating point but an otherwise limited instruction set.

System/360 Model 65 operator's console, with register value lamps and toggle switches (middle of picture) and "emergency pull" switch (upper right).

A succession of high-end machines included the 67 (1966, mentioned below, briefly anticipated as the 64 and 66[5]), 85 (1969), 91 (1967, anticipated as the 92), 95 (1968), and 195 (1971). The 85 design was intermediate between the System/360 line and the follow-on System/370 and was the basis for the 370/165. There was a System/370 version of the 195, but it did not include Dynamic Address Translation.

The implementations differed substantially, using different native data path widths, presence or absence of microcode, yet were extremely compatible. Except where specifically documented, the models were architecturally compatible. The 91, for example, was designed for scientific computing and

This image of the System/360 Model 91 was taken by NASA sometime in the late 60s.

provided out-of-order instruction execution (and could yield "imprecise interrupts" if a program trap occurred while several instructions were being read), but lacked the decimal instruction set used in commercial applications. New features could be added without violating architectural definitions: the 65 had a dual-processor version (M65MP) with extensions for inter-CPU signalling; the 85 introduced cache memory. Models 44, 75, 91, 95, and 195 were implemented with hardwired logic, rather than microcoded as all other models.

The S/360-67, announced in August 1965, was the first production IBM system to offer dynamic address translation hardware to support time-sharing. "DAT" is now more commonly referred to as an MMU. An experimental one-off unit was built based on a model 40. Before the 67, IBM had announced models 64 and 66, DAT versions of the 60 and 62, but they were almost immediately replaced by the 67 at the same time that the 60 and 62 were replaced by the 65. DAT hardware would reappear in the S/370 series in 1972, though it was initially absent from the series. Like the 65 to which it was closely related, the 67 also had a dual-CPU implementation.

All System/360 models were withdrawn from marketing by the end of 1977.

Backward compatibility

IBM's existing customers had a large investment in software that executed on second generation machines. Many models offered the option of emulation of the customer's previous computer (e.g. the IBM 1400 series on a 360-30 or the IBM 7094 on a 360-65) using a combination of special hardware,[6] special microcode and an emulation program that used the emulation instructions to simulate the target system, so that old programs could run on the new machine. However, customers had to halt the computer and load the emulation program.[7] The 360/85 and later System/370 retained the emulation options, but allowed them to be executed under operating system control alongside native programs.[8]

Successors and variants

The S/360 (excepting the 360/20) was replaced by the compatible System/370 range in 1970 and 360/20 users were targeted to move to the IBM System/3. (The idea of a major breakthrough with FS technology was dropped in the mid-1970s for cost-effectiveness and continuity reasons.) Later compatible IBM systems include the 3090, the ES/9000 family, 9672 (System/390 family), the zSeries, System z9, System z10 and IBM zEnterprise System.

Computers that were mostly[9] identical or compatible in terms of the machine code or architecture of the System/360 included Amdahl's 470 family (and its successors), Hitachi mainframes, the UNIVAC 9200/9300/9400 series, the English Electric System 4, and the RCA Spectra 70 series, which was sold to what was then UNIVAC to become the UNIVAC 90/60 and later releases. The Soviet Union produced an S/360 clone named the ES EVM.

The IBM 5100 portable computer, introduced in 1975, offered an option to execute the System/360's APL.SV programming language through a hardware emulator. IBM used this approach in order to avoid the costs and delay in creating a version of APL specific to the 5100.

Special radiation-hardened and otherwise somewhat modified S/360s, in the form of the System/4 Pi avionics computer, are used in several fighter and bomber jet aircraft. In the complete 32-bit AP-101 version, 4 Pi machines are used as the replicated computing nodes of the fault-tolerant Space Shuttle computer system (in five nodes). The U.S. Federal Aviation Administration operated the IBM 9020, a special cluster of modified System/360s for air traffic control, from 1970 until the 1990s. (Some 9020 software is apparently still used via emulation on newer hardware.)

Technical description

Influential features

The System/360 introduced a number of industry standards to the marketplace, such as:

- The 8-bit byte (against financial pressure during development to reduce the byte to 4 or 6 bits), rather than adopting the 7030 concept of accessing bytes of variable size at arbitrary bit addresses.
- Byte-addressable memory (as opposed to bit-addressable or word-addressable memory)
- 32-bit words
- The bus and tag I/O channel standardized in FIPS-60[10]
- Commercial use of microcoded CPUs
- The IBM Floating Point Architecture (until superseded by the IEEE 754-1985 floating-point standard, 20 years later)
- The EBCDIC character set[11]
- Nine track magnetic tape

IBM System 360-20 Microcode TROS

Architectural overview

The System/360 series had a computer system architecture specification.[12] [12] [12] This specification does not make any assumptions on the implementation itself, but rather describes the interfaces and the expected behavior of an implementation. The architecture describes mandatory interfaces that must be available on all implementations and optional interfaces which may or may not be implemented.

Some of the aspects of this architecture are:

- Big endian byte ordering
- A processor with
  - 16 32-bit General purpose registers (R0-R15)
  - A 64-bit Program status word (PSW) which describes (among other things)
    - Interrupt masks
    - Privilege states
    - A condition code
    - A 24-bit instruction address
  - An interruption mechanism, maskable and unmaskable interruption classes and subclasses
  - An instruction set. Each instruction is wholly described and also defines the conditions under which an exception is recognized in the form of program interruption.
- A memory (called storage) subsystem with
  - 8 bits per byte
  - A special processor communication area starting at address 0
  - 24-bit addressing
- Manual control operations that allow
  - A bootstrap process (a process called Initial Program Load or IPL)
  - Operator-initiated interrupts
  - Resetting the system
  - Basic debugging facilities
  - Manual display and modifications of the system's state (memory and processor)
- An Input/Output mechanism - which does not describe the devices themselves

Some of the optional features are:

- Binary-coded decimal instructions
- Floating point instructions
- Timing facilities (interval timer)
- Key-controlled memory protection

All models of System/360, except for the Model 20, implemented that specification.

Binary arithmetic and logical operations are performed as register-to-register and as memory-to-register/register-to-memory as a standard feature. If the Commercial Instruction Set option was installed, packed decimal arithmetic could be performed as memory-to-memory with some memory-to-register operations. The Scientific Instruction Set feature, if installed, provided access to four floating point registers that could be programmed for either 32-bit or 64-bit floating point operations. The Models 85 and 195 could also operate on 128-bit extended-precision floating point numbers stored in pairs of floating point registers, and software provided emulation in other models. The System/360 used an 8-bit byte, 32-bit word, 64-bit double-word, and 4-bit nibble. Machine instructions had operators with operands, which could contain register numbers or memory addresses. This complex combination of instruction options resulted in a variety of instruction lengths and formats.

Memory addressing was accomplished using a base-plus-displacement scheme, with registers 1 through F (15). A displacement was encoded in 12 bits, thus allowing a 4096-byte displacement (0-4095), as the offset from the address put in a base register. Register 0 could not be used as a base register, as "0" was reserved to indicate an address in the first 4 KB of memory. This permitted initial execution of the interrupt routines, since base registers would not necessarily be set to 0 during the first few instruction cycles of an interrupt routine. It isn't needed for IPL ("Initial Program Load" or boot), as one can always clear a register without the need to save it.

With the exception of the Model 67,[13] all addresses were real memory addresses. Virtual memory was not available in most IBM mainframes until the System/370 series. The Model 67 introduced a virtual memory architecture which was used by MTS, CP-67, and TSS/360, but not by IBM's mainline System/360 operating systems.

The System/360 machine-code instructions are 2 (no memory operands), 4 (one operand), or 6 bytes (two operands) long. Instructions are always situated on 2-byte boundaries.

Operations like the MVC (Move-Character) (Hex: D2) can only move at most 256 bytes of information. Moving more than 256 bytes of data required multiple MVC operations. (The System/370 series introduced a family of more powerful instructions such as the MVCL "Move-Character-Long" instruction, which allows 16 MB to be moved at once.)

An operand is two bytes long, typically representing an address as a 4-bit nibble denoting a base register and a 12-bit displacement relative to the contents of that register, in the range 000–FFF (shown here as hexadecimal numbers). The address corresponding to that operand is the contents of the specified general-purpose register plus the displacement. For example, an MVC instruction that moves 256 bytes (with length code 255 in hexadecimal as FF) from base register 7, plus displacement 000, to base register 8, plus displacement 001, would be coded as the 6-byte instruction "D2FF 8001 7000" (operator/length/address1/address2).

The System/360 was designed to separate the "system state" from the "problem state". This provided a basic level of security and recoverability from programming errors. Problem (user) programs could not modify data or program storage associated with the system state. Addressing, data, or operation exception errors caused the system state to be entered through a controlled routine allowing the operating system to attempt to correct or terminate the program in error. Similarly, certain processor hardware errors could be recovered through the "machine check" routines.

Channels

Peripherals interfaced to the system via *channels*. A channel was a specialized processor with the instruction set optimized for transferring data between a peripheral and main memory. In modern terms, this could be compared to direct memory access (DMA).

There were initially two types of channels; byte-multiplexer channels, for connecting "slow speed" devices such as card readers and punches, line printers, and communications controllers, and selector channels for connecting high speed devices, such as disk drives, tape drives, data cells and drums. Every S/360 (except for the Model 20, which was not a standard S/360) had a byte-multiplexer channel and 1 or more selector channels. The smaller models (up to the model 50) had integrated channels, while for the larger models (model 65 and above) the channels were large separate units in separate cabinets, such as the IBM 2860 and 2870.

The byte-multiplexer channel was able to handle I/O to/from several devices simultaneously at the device's highest rated speeds, hence the name, as it multiplexed I/O from those devices onto a single data path to main memory. Devices connected to a byte-multiplexer channel were configured to operate in 1-byte, 2-byte, 4-byte, or "burst" mode. The larger "blocks" of data were used to handle progressively faster devices. For example, a 2501 card reader operating at 600 cards per minute would be in 1-byte mode, while a 1403-N1 printer would be in burst mode. Also, the byte-multiplexer channel had an optional sub-selector section that would accommodate tape drives. The byte-multiplexor's channel address was typically "0" and the sub-selector addresses were from "C0" to "FF." Thus, tape drives on S/360 were commonly addressed at 0C0-0C7. Other common byte-multiplexer addresses were: 00A: 2501 Card Reader, 00C/00D: 2540 Reader/Punch, 00E/00F: 1403-N1 Printers, 010-013: 3211 Printers, 020-0BF: 2701/2703 Telecommunications Units. These addresses are still commonly used in z/VM virtual machines.

The S/360 models 30, 40, and 50 had an integrated 1052-7 console that was usually addressed as 01F, however, this was not connected to the byte-multiplexer channel, but rather, had a direct internal connection to the mainframe.

Selector channels enabled I/O to high speed devices. These storage devices were attached to a control unit and then to the channel. The control unit enabled clusters of devices to be attached to the channels. On higher speed S/360 models, multiple selector channels, which could operate simultaneously or in parallel, improved overall performance.

Control units were connected to the channels with gray "bus and tag" cable pairs. The bus cables carried the address and data information and the tag cables identified what data was on the bus. The general configuration of a channel was to connect the devices in a chain, like this: Mainframe—Control Unit X—Control Unit Y—Control Unit Z. Each control unit was assigned a "capture range" of addresses that it serviced. For example, control unit X might capture addresses 40-4F, control unit Y: C0-DF, and control unit Z: 80-9F. The capture ranges had to be a multiple of 8, 16, 32, 64, or 128 devices and be aligned on appropriate boundaries. Each control unit in turn had one or more devices attached to it. For example, you could have control unit Y with 6 disks, that would be addressed as C0-C5.

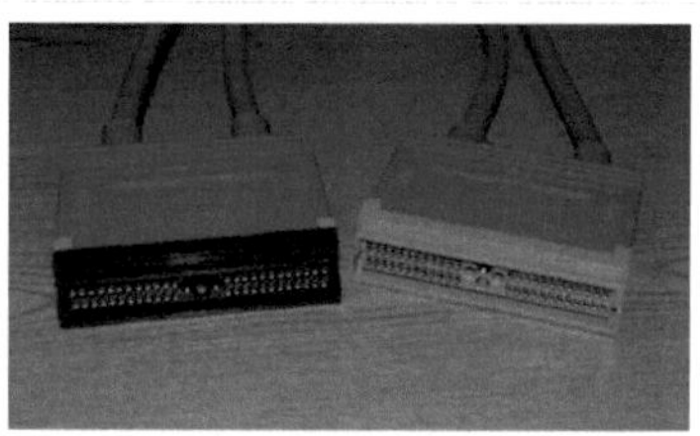

Bus & tag cable

The cable ordering of the control units on the channel was also significant. Each control unit was "strapped" as High or Low priority. When a device selection was sent out on a mainframe's channel, the selection was sent from X->Y->Z->Y->X. If the control unit was "high" then the selection was checked in the outbound direction, if "low" then the inbound direction. Thus, control unit X was either 1st or 5th, Y was either 2nd or 4th, and Z was 3rd in line. It was also possible to have multiple channels attached to a control unit from the same or multiple mainframes, thus providing a rich high-performance, multiple-access, and backup capability.

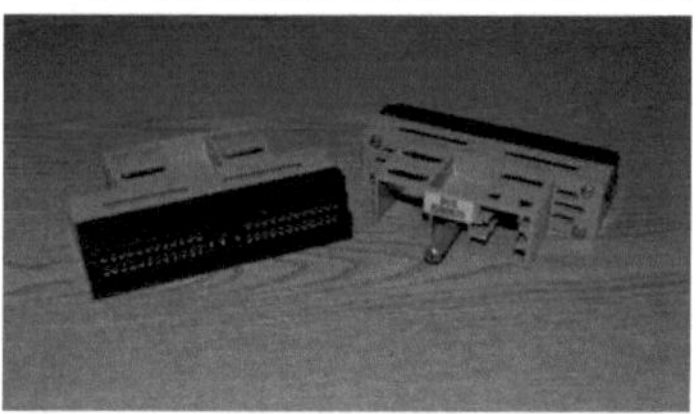

Bus & tag terminators

Typically the total cable length of a channel was limited to 200 feet, less being preferred. Each control unit accounted for about 10 "feet" of the 200-foot limit.

Block multiplexer channel

IBM introduced a new type of I/O channel on the 360/85 and 360/195: the 2880 block multiplexer channel. The channel allowed a device to suspend a channel program, pending the completion of an I/O operation and thus to free the channel for use by another device. The initial use for this was the 2305 fixed-head disk, which had 8 "exposures" (alias addresses) and rotational position sensing (RPS).

These channels could support either standard 1.5 MB/second connections or, with the 2-byte interface feature, 3 MB/second; the later used one tag cable and two bus cables.

Basic hardware components

Being somewhat uncertain of the reliability and availability of the then new monolithic integrated circuits, IBM chose instead to design custom hybrid integrated circuits using discrete flip chip mounted glass encapsulated transistors and diodes with silk screened resistors on a ceramic substrate, then either encapsulated in plastic or covered with a metal lid. Several of these were then mounted on a small multi-layer printed circuit board to make a "Solid Logic Technology" (SLT) module. Each SLT module had a socket on one edge that plugged into pins on the computer's backplane (the reverse of how most other company's modules were mounted).

Operating system software

The smaller S/360 models used Basic Operating System/360 (BOS/360), Tape Operating System (TOS/360), or Disk Operating System/360 (DOS/360, which evolved into DOS/VS, DOS/VSE, VSE/AF, VSE/SP, VSE/ESA, and then z/VSE).

The larger S/360 models used Operating System/360 (OS/360): Primary Control Program (PCP), Multiprogramming with a Fixed number of Tasks (MFT), which evolved into OS/VS1, and

SLT card frame. Image from The Corestore [14].

Multiprogramming with a Variable number of Tasks (MVT), which evolved into MVS. MVT took a long time to develop into a usable system, and the less ambitious MFT was widely used. PCP was used on intermediate machines; the final releases of OS/360 included only MFT and MVT.

When it announced the S/360-67 in August 1965, IBM also announced TSS/360 (Time-Sharing System) for delivery at the same time as the 67. TSS/360, a response to Multics, was an ambitious project that included many advanced features. It never worked properly, was delayed, canceled, reinstated, and finally canceled again in 1971. It was replaced by CP-67, MTS (Michigan Terminal System), TSO (Time Sharing Option for OS/360), or one of several other time-sharing systems.

CP-67, the original virtual machine system, was also known as CP/CMS. CP/67 was developed outside the IBM mainstream at IBM's Cambridge Scientific Center, in cooperation with MIT researchers. CP/CMS eventually won wide acceptance, and led to the development of VM/370 (aka VM/CMS) and today's z/VM.

The S/360 Model 20 offered a simplified and rarely used tape-based system called TPS (Tape Processing System), and also DPS (Disk Processing System) that provided support for the 2311 disk drive. TPS could run on a machine with 8K of memory, and DPS required 12 K, which was pretty hefty for a Model 20. Many customers ran quite happily with 4 K and CPS (Card Processing System).

With TPS and DOS, the card reader was used (a) to define the stack of jobs to be run (Job Control Language), and (b) to feed in transaction data, like customer payments. But the operating system was held on tape or disk, and results (master files!) could also be stored on the tapes or hard drives. Stacked job processing became an exciting possibility for the small but adventurous computer user.

A little known and little used suite of 80 column punched-card utility programs known as Basic Programming Support (BPS) (jocularly: Barely Programming Support) was available for the S/360-30. It was a precursor of TOS on the Model 30.

Component names

IBM created a new naming system for the new components created for System/360, although well-known old names, like IBM 1403 and IBM 1052, were retained. In this new naming system, components were given four-digit numbers starting with 2. The second digit described the type of component, as follows:

20xx: Arithmetic processors, for example the IBM 2030, which was the CPU for the IBM System/360 Model 30.

21xx: Power supplies and other equipment intimately associated with processors, for example the IBM 2167 Configuration Unit.

22xx: Visual output devices, for example the IBM 2250 and IBM 2260 CRT displays, and the IBM 2203 line printer for the System/360 model 20.

23xx: Direct-access storage devices, for example the IBM 2311 and IBM 2314 disk drives, the IBM 2321 Data Cell;
Main storage such as the IBM 2361 Large Capacity Storage (Core Storage, Large Core Storage or LCS) and the IBM 2365 Processor Storage.

24xx: Magnetic tape drives, for example the IBM 2401, IBM 2405 and IBM 2415.

25xx: Punched card handling equipment, for example the IBM 2501 (card reader), IBM 2520 (card punch); IBM 2540 (reader/punch) and IBM 2560 (Multi-Function Card Machine or MFCM).

26xx: Paper tape handling equipment, for example the IBM 2671 paper tape reader.

27xx: Communications equipment, for example the IBM 2701, IBM 2705, IBM 2741 interactive terminal and the IBM 2780 batch terminal.

28xx: Channels and controllers, for example the IBM 2821 Control Unit, IBM 2841 and IBM 2844.

29xx: Miscellaneous devices, for example the IBM 2914 Data Channel Switch and the IBM 2944 Data Channel Repeater.

Peripherals

IBM developed a new family of peripheral equipment for the S/360, carrying over a few from its older 1400 series. Interfaces were standardized, allowing greater flexibility to mix and match processors, controllers and peripherals than in the earlier product lines.

In addition, the S/360 computers could use certain peripherals that were originally developed for earlier computers. These earlier peripherals used a different numbering system, such as the IBM 1403 chain printer. The 1403, an extremely reliable device which had already earned a reputation as a workhorse, was sold as the 1403-N1 when adapted for the System/360.

Also available were optical character recognition (OCR) readers 1287 and 1288.

Most small systems were sold with an IBM 1052-7 as the console typewriter. This was tightly integrated into the CPU — the keyboard would physically lock under program control. Certain high-end machines could optionally be purchased with a 2250 graphical display, costing upwards of US $100,000. The 360/85 used a 5450 display console that was not compatible with anything else in the line; the later 3066 console for the 370/165 and 370/168 used the same basic display design as the 360/85.

Direct access storage devices (DASD)

The first disk drives for the 360 were IBM 2302s[15] :60-65 and IBM 2311s. The 156 kB/second 2302 was based on the earlier 1302 and was available as a model 3 with two 112.79 MB modules or as a model 4 with four such modules.

The 2311, with a removable 1316 disk pack, was based on the IBM 1311 and had a theoretical capacity of 7.2 MB, although actual capacity varied with record design.[16] :31 (When used with a 360/20, the 1316 pack was formatted into fixed-length sectors, giving a maximum capacity of 5.4MB.)

In 1966, the first 2314s shipped. This device had up to eight usable disk drives with an integral control unit; there were nine drives, but one had to be reserved as a spare. Each drive used a removable 2316 disk pack with a capacity of nearly 28 MB. The disk packs for the 2311 and 2314 were *physically* large by today's standards — e.g., the 1316 disk pack was about 14 in (**unknown operator: u'strong'** cm) in diameter and had six platters stacked on a central spindle. The top and bottom

IBM 2311 disk drive.

outside platters did not store data. Data were recorded on the inner sides of the top and bottom platters and both sides of the inner platters, providing 10 recording surfaces. The 10 read/write heads moved together across the surfaces of the platters which were formatted with 203 concentric tracks. To reduce the amount of head movement (seeking), data was written in a virtual cylinder from inside top platter down to inside bottom platter. These disks were not usually formatted with fixed-sized sectors as are today's hard drives (though this *was* done with CP/CMS). Rather, most S/360 I/O software could customize the length of the data record (variable-length records), as was the case with magnetic tapes.

Some of the most powerful early S/360s used high-speed head-per-track drum storage devices. The 3,500 RPM 2301,[17] which replaced the 7320, was part of the original S/360 announcement, with a capacity of 4Mb. The 303.8 kB/second IBM 2303[15] :74-76 was announced on January 31, 1966, with a capacity of 3.913 MB. These were the only drums announced for the S/360 and S/370, and their niche was later filled by fixed-head disks.

IBM 2314 Disk Drives and IBM 2540 Card Reader/Punch at the University of Michigan.

The 6,000 RPM 2305 appeared in 1970, with capacities of 5 Mb (2305-1) or 11 Mb (2305-2) per module.[18] [19] Although these devices did not have large capacity, their speed and transfer rates made them attractive for high-performance needs. A typical use was overlay linkage (e.g. for OS and application subroutines) for program sections written to alternate in the same memory regions. Fixed head disks and drums were particularly effective as paging devices on the early virtual memory systems. The 2305, although often called a "drum" was actually a head-per-track disk device, with 12 recording surfaces and a data transfer rate up to 3 megabytes per second.

Rarely seen was the IBM 2321 Data Cell,[20] a mechanically complex device that contained multiple magnetic strips to hold data; strips could be randomly accessed, placed upon a cylinder-shaped drum for read/write operations; then returned to an internal storage cartridge. The IBM Data Cell [noodle picker] was among several IBM trademarked "speedy" mass online direct-access storage peripherals (reincarnated in recent years as "virtual tape" and automated tape librarian peripherals). The 2321 file had a capacity of 400 MB, at the time when the 2311 disk drive only had 7.2 MB. The IBM Data Cell was proposed to fill cost/capacity/speed gap between magnetic tapes—which had high capacity with relatively low cost per stored byte—and disks, which had higher expense per byte. Some installations also found the electromechanical operation less dependable and opted for less mechanical forms of direct-access storage.

The Model 44 was unique in offering an integrated single-disk drive as a standard feature. This drive used the 2315 "ramkit" cartridge and provided 1171200 bytes of storage.[21] :11

Tape drives

The 2400 tape drives consisted of a combined drive and control unit, plus individual 1/2" tape drives attached. With the 360, IBM switched from IBM 7 track to 9 track tape format. 2400 drives could be purchased that read and wrote 7 track tapes for compatibility with the older IBM 729 tape drives. In 1967, a slower and cheaper pair of tape drives with integrated control unit was introduced: the 2415. In 1968, the IBM 2420 tape system was released, offering much higher data rates, self-threading tape operation and 1600bpi packing density. It remained in the product line until 1979.

IBM 2401 Tape Drives

Unit record devices

- Punched card devices included the 2501 card reader and the 2540 card reader punch. Virtually every S/360 had a 2540. The 2560 MFCM ("Multi-Function Card Machine") reader/sorter/punch, listed above, was for the Model 20 only. It had notorious reliability problems (earning humorous acroymns often involving "...Card Muncher" or "Mal-Function Card Machine).
- Line printers were the IBM 1403 and the slower IBM 1443.
- A paper tape reader, the IBM 2671, was introduced in 1964. It had a rated speed of 1,000 cps. There were also a paper tape reader and paper tape punch from an earlier era, available only as RPQs (Request Price Quotation). The 1054 (reader) and 1055 (punch), which were carried forward (like the 1052 console typewriter) from the IBM 1050 Teleprocessing System. All these devices operated at a maximum of 15.5 characters per second. The paper tape punch from the IBM 1080 System was also available by RPQ, but at a prohibitively expensive price.

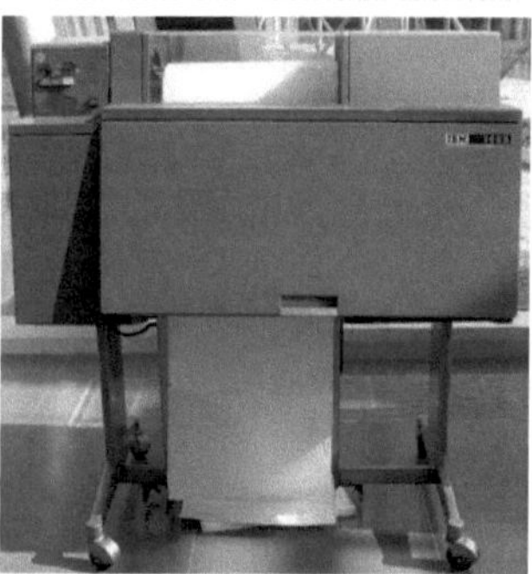

IBM 1403 line printer.

- Optical Character Recognition (OCR) devices 1287 and latter the 1288 were available on the 360's. The 1287 could read handwritten numerals, some OCR fonts, and cash register OCR paper tape reels. The 1288 'page reader' could handle up to legal size OCR font typewritten pages, as well as handwritten numerals. Both of these OCR devices employed a 'flying spot' scanning principle, with the raster scan provided by a large CRT, and the reflected light density changes were picked up by a high gain Photo Multiplier tube.
- MICR (Magnetic Ink Character Recognition) was provided by the IBM 1412 and 1419 Cheque Sorters, with Magnetic Ink Printing (for cheque books) on 1445 Printers (a modified 1443 that used an MICR ribbon). 1412/1419 and 1445 were mainly used by Banking Institutions.

Remaining machines

Few of these machines remain. Despite being sold or leased in very large numbers for a mainframe system of its era, only a few System/360 computers are known to exist today, none of which are in working condition. Most machines were scrapped when they could no longer profitably be leased, partly for the gold and other precious metal content of their circuits, but mainly to keep these machines from competing with IBM's newer computers, such as the System/370. As with all classic mainframe systems, complete System/360 computers were prohibitively large to be held in storage, and too expensive to maintain. The Smithsonian Institution owns a System/360 Model 65, although it is no longer on public display. The Computer History Museum in Mountain View, CA has a non-working System/360 Model 30 on display, as does the Museum of Transport and Technology (Motat) in Auckland, New Zealand and the Vienna University of Technology in Austria. The University of Western Australia has a complete System/360 in storage at its Shenton Park warehouse. The IBM museum in Sindelfingen has two S/360s (a Model 20 and a Model 91 floating point machine). The control panel of the most complex System/360 model type built, the FAA IBM 9020, comprising up to 12 System/360 model 65s and System/360 model 50s in its maximum configuration is on display in the Computer Science department of Stanford University as IBM 360 display and Stanford Big Iron [22]. It was manufactured in 1971 and decommissioned in 1993. The IBM Endicott History and Heritage Center in Endicott, NY has a non-working System/360 and an associated 2401 magnetic tape drive on display.

See also

- History of IBM
- List of IBM products
- Dr. Gene Amdahl (architect)
- Dr. Gerrit Blaauw (architect)
- Dr. Fred Brooks (System/360 project manager)
- Bob Evans (computer scientist)

Notes

[1] IBM System/360 Dates and Characteristics (http://www-03.ibm.com/ibm/history/exhibits/mainframe/mainframe_FS360.html)

[2] System 360/30 announcement (http://www-03.ibm.com/ibm/history/exhibits/mainframe/mainframe_PP2030.html)

[3] "System/360 Announcement" (press release), IBM Data Processing Division, April 7, 1964, webpage: IBM-PR360 (http://www-03.ibm. com/ibm/history/exhibits/mainframe/mainframe_PR360.html): states cycle time from "millionth-of-a-second to only 200 billionths-of-a-second" and "memory capacity ranges from 8,000 characters of information to more than 8,000,000".

[4] An Appreciation - John R. Opel, posted on www.ibm.com (http://www.ibm.com/ibm/us/en/johnopel.html)

[5] DIGITAL COMPUTER NEWSLETTER (http://www.dtic.mil/cgi-bin/GetTRDoc?Location=U2&doc=GetTRDoc.pdf& AD=AD0694645), Office of Naval Research, Mathematical Sciences Division, July 1965--pages 5-6: IBM System/360 time-sharing computers

[6] IBM (February 1971), *System/370 Model 165 Theory of Operation (Volume 8) 709/7090/7094/7094-II Compatability Ferature*, Second Edition, SY77-6835-0.

[7] IBM (April 1964), *System/360, Model 30 1401 Compatibility Feature* (http://www.bitsavers.org/pdf/ibm/360/1401_emulator/ A24-3255-1_Model30_1401_Compatibility_Apr64.pdf), A24-3255-1, , "Mode status (System/360, Model 30, mode or 1401 compatibility mode) is set during the read-in of the compatibility initialization deck."

[8] IBM (November 1971), *Emulating the IBM 7094 on the IBM Models 85 and 165 using OS/360 Program Number for M/85: 360C-EU-734 Program Number for M/165: 360C-EU-740 OS Release 20*, Third Edition, GC27-6951-2

[9] The RCA Spectra 70 had radically different architecture for interrupts and I/O. There were compatibility packages to allow operating systems for the S/360 to run on a Spectra/70 and vice versa.

[10] NTIS (1979), *I/O Channel Interface*, National Technical Information Service, FIPSPUB60

[11] IBM was a major advocate of the ASCII standardization, supporting the approval of the American Standard Code for Information Interchange, ASA X3.4-1963. This code was first implemented in the Teletype Model 33 machines used in American Telephone & Telegraph's TWX (TeletypeWriter eXchange) network. A proposed American National Standard for the representation of ASCII in 80-column, 12-row punched cards was in the approval process when System/360 was announced. In the System/360 architecture bit 12 of the Program status word (PSW), see IBM Corp (1964), p.70, controlled selection of the EBCDIC or the ASCII mode signed decimal data as

described on p.35. Thus the System/360 processor architecture provided support of this proposed ASCII standard in anticipation of its approval. When the user community rejected this proposed standard, the requisite peripheral devices were never made available and this System/360 capability was not included in System/370. Bit 12 of the PSW was redefined to switch between System/360 and System/370 modes.

These second-generation systems supported "national use" characters in the IBM Binary-Coded Decimal standard to accommodate the accented characters in the alphabets of French speaking Canada, Central and South America and Western Europe. See Western Latin character sets (computing) for a discussion of the problems involved and the various solutions, including EBCDIC, that have been used over the years. When designing System/360, ASCII had yet to be expanded for international use, a work that began later under the name Unicode.

[12] IBM (1964), *IBM System/360 Principles of Operation* (http://bitsavers.org/pdf/ibm/360/princOps/A22-6821-0_360PrincOps.pdf), A22-6821-0, .

[13] IBM (February 1972), *IBM System/360 Model 67 Functional Characteristics* (http://bitsavers.org/pdf/ibm/360/funcChar/GA27-2719-2_360-67_funcChar.pdf), Third Edition, GA27-2719-2, .

[14] http://www.corestore.org

[15] IBM (December 1969). *IBM System/360 Component Descriptions - 2841 and Associated DASD* (http://bitsavers.org/pdf/ibm/28xx/2841/GA26-5988-7_2841_DASD_Component_Descr_Dec69.pdf). Eighth Edition. GA26-5988-7. .

[16] http://www.bitsavers.org/pdf/ibm/dasd/A26-5988-0_2841_2311_2321_7320_Descr.pdf

[17] IBM 2301 Drum Storage (http://www.columbia.edu/acis/history/drum.html), Columbia University Computing History

[18] IBM 2305 product announcement (http://ed-thelen.org/comp-hist/IBM-ProdAnn/2305.pdf)

[19] IBM (November 1980), *Reference Manual for IBM 2835 Storage Control and IBM 2305 Fixed Head Storage Module*, Fifth Edition, GA26-1689-4.

[20] The IBM 2321 Data Cell Drive (http://www.columbia.edu/acis/history/datacell.html), Columbia University Computing History

[21] IBM System/360 Model 44 Functional Characteristics (http://www.bitsavers.org/pdf/ibm/360/funcChar/A22-6875-5_360-44_funcChar.pdf)

[22] http://infolab.stanford.edu/pub/voy/museum/pictures/display/3-1.htm

References

- Emerson W. Pugh, Lyle R. Johnson, John H. Palmer, *IBM's 360 and Early 370 Systems* (http://books.google.com/books?id=MFGj_PT_clIC&printsec=frontcover&dq=IBM's+360), Cambridge: MIT Press, 1991, ISBN 0-262-16123-0. This is the definitive reference work on the early history of the S/360 and early S/370 family.
- IBM Corp (1964). *IBM System/360 Principles of Operation* (http://bitsavers.org/pdf/ibm/360/princOps/A22-6821-0_360PrincOps.pdf). Poughkeepsie, NY: IBM Systems Reference Library, File No. S360-01, Form A22-6821-0.

External links

From the IBM Journal of Research and Development

- *Architecture of the IBM System/360* (http://www.research.ibm.com/journal/rd/441/amdahl.pdf) — By S/360 architects Gene Amdahl (HW), Fred Brooks (OS), and G. A. Blaauw (HW)
- *Solid Logic Technology* (http://www.research.ibm.com/journal/rd/082/ibmrd0802D.pdf) — By E. M. Davis, W. E. Harding, R. S. Schwartz and J. J. Corning

From IBM Systems Journal

- Blaauw, G. A., and Brooks, F.P., Jr., "The Structure of System/360, Part I-Outline of the Logical Structure" (http://domino.research.ibm.com/tchjr/journalindex.nsf/d9f0a910ab8b637485256bc80066a393/95dc427e3fd3024a85256bfa006859f7?OpenDocument), *IBM Systems Journal*, vol. 3, no. 2, pp. 119–135, 1964.
- Stevens, W. Y., The structure of SYSTEM/360, Part II: System implementations" (http://domino.research.ibm.com/tchjr/journalindex.nsf/a3807c5b4823c53f85256561006324be/62abd917761627ae85256bfa006859f8?OpenDocument), *IBM Systems Journal*, Volume 3, Number 2/3, Page 136 (1964)

- Amdahl, G. M., "The structure of SYSTEM/360, Part III: Processing unit design considerations" (http://domino. research.ibm.com/tchjr/journalindex.nsf/a3807c5b4823c53f85256561006324be/ 361bf4987071716885256bfa006859f9?OpenDocument), *IBM Systems Journal*, Volume 3, Number 2/3, Page 144 (1964)
- Padegs, A., "The structure of SYSTEM/360, Part IV: Channel design considerations" (http://domino.research. ibm.com/tchjr/journalindex.nsf/a3807c5b4823c53f85256561006324be/ 732a20f6f631903d85256bfa006859fa?OpenDocument), *IBM Systems Journal*, Volume 3, Number 2/3, Page 165 (1964)
- Blaauw, G.A., " The structure of SYSTEM/360, Part V: Multisystem organization" (http://domino.research. ibm.com/tchjr/journalindex.nsf/a3807c5b4823c53f85256561006324be/ f0fd35ae8745ac4b85256bfa006859fb?OpenDocument), *IBM Systems Journal*, Volume 3, Number 2/3, Page 181 (1964)
- Tucker, S. G., "Microprogram control for SYSTEM/360" (http://domino.research.ibm.com/tchjr/ journalindex.nsf/a3807c5b4823c53f85256561006324be/ 758c1e6a8a3e5d0285256bfa00685a2f?OpenDocument) *IBM Systems Journal*, Volume 6, Number 4, pp. 222–241 (1967)

General

- IBM's announcement of the System/360 (http://www-03.ibm.com/ibm/history/exhibits/mainframe/ mainframe_PR360.html)
- Generations of the IBM 360/370/3090/390 (http://www.beagle-ears.com/lars/engineer/comphist/ibm360. htm) by Lars Poulsen with multiple links and references
- Several photos (http://www.eecis.udel.edu/~mills/gallery/gallery8.html) of a dual processor IBM 360/67 at the University of Michigan's academic Computing Center in the late 1960s or early 1970s are included in Dave Mills' article describing the Michigan Terminal System (MTS)
- Pictures of an [[IBM System/360-67|IBM S/360-67 (http://history.cs.ncl.ac.uk/anniversaries/40th/images/ ibm360_672/index.html)] at Newcastle (UK) University]
- Video of a two-hour lecture and panel discussion (http://www.youtube.com/watch?v=8c0_Lzb1CJw) entitled *The IBM System/360 Revolution*, from the Computer History Museum on 2004-04-07
- scanned manuals of IBM System/360 (http://www.bitsavers.org/pdf/ibm/360/) — at bitsavers.org
- Description of a large IBM System/360 model 75 installation at JPL (http://tmo.jpl.nasa.gov/progress_report2/ VII/VIIV.PDF)
- "The Beginning of I.T. Civilization - IBM's System/360 Mainframe" by Mike Kahn (http://www-07.ibm.com/ systems/tw/z/download/clipper_mainframe_at40.pdf)
- Illustrations from "Introduction to IBM Data Processing Systems", 1968 (http://www.beagle-ears.com/lars/ engineer/comphist/c20-1684/): contains photographs of IBM System/360 computers and peripherals
- Dates of announcement, first ship and withdrawal of all models of the IBM System/360 (http://www-03.ibm. com/ibm/history/exhibits/mainframe/mainframe_FS360.html)
- IBM System 360 RPG Debugging Template and Keypunch Card (http://www.gutenberg.org/ebooks/37504)

This article is based on material taken from the Free On-line Dictionary of Computing prior to 1 November 2008 and incorporated under the "relicensing" terms of the GFDL, version 1.3 or later.

IBM_7030_Stretch

The **IBM 7030**, also known as **Stretch**, was IBM's first transistorized supercomputer. The first one was delivered to Los Alamos National Laboratory in 1961.

Originally priced at $13.5 million, its failure to meet its aggressive performance estimates forced the price to be dropped to only $7.78 million and its withdrawal from sales to customers beyond those having already negotiated contracts. Even though the 7030 was much slower than expected, it was the fastest computer in the world from 1961 until the first CDC 6600 became operational in 1964.

Development history

Dr. Edward Teller at the University of California Radiation Laboratory in Livermore, California wanted a new scientific system for three-dimensional hydrodynamic calculations. Proposals were requested for this new system, to be called *Livermore Automatic Reaction Calculator* or LARC, from both IBM and UNIVAC. Expected to cost roughly $2.5 million and running at one to two MIPS, delivery was to be two to three years after the contract was signed.

IBM 7030 maintenance console at the *Musée des Arts et Métiers*, Paris

At IBM, a small team at Poughkeepsie including John Griffith and Gene Amdahl worked on the design proposal. Just after they finished and were about to present the proposal, Ralph Palmer stopped them and said, "It's a mistake." The proposed design would have been built with either point-contact transistors or surface barrier transistors, both likely to be soon outperformed by the then newly invented diffusion transistors. The team showed Livermore the proposed design to illustrate the kind of system IBM was capable of building but said, "We are not going to build that machine for you; we want to build something better! We do not know precisely what it will take but we think it will   be   another million dollars and another year, and we do not know how fast it will run but we would like to shoot for ten million instructions per second."

In May 1955, IBM lost the bid because of this unanticipated change of direction in their proposal. UNIVAC, the dominant computer manufacturer at the time, had won the contract for LARC, now called the *Livermore Automatic Research Computer.*

In September 1955, fearing that Los Alamos National Laboratory might also order a LARC, IBM submitted a preliminary proposal for a high-performance binary computer based on the improved design that Livermore had rejected, which they received with interest. In January 1956, Project Stretch was formally initiated.

IBM 7030 maintenance console at the *Musée des Arts et Métiers*, Paris

In November 1956, IBM won the contract for a binary computer with the aggressive performance goal of a "speed at least 100 times the IBM 704" (i.e. 4 MIPS) to the Los Alamos Scientific Laboratory. Delivery was slated for 1960.

During design, it proved necessary to reduce the clock speeds, making it clear that Stretch could not meet its aggressive performance goals, but estimates of performance ranged from 60 to 100 times the IBM 704. In 1960, the price of $13.5 million was set for the IBM 7030.

In 1961, actual benchmarks indicated that the performance of the IBM 7030 was only about 30 times the IBM 704 (i.e. 1.2 MIPS), causing considerable embarrassment for IBM. In May 1961, Tom Watson announced a price cut of all 7030s under negotiation to $7.78 million and immediate withdrawal of the product from further sales.

Its floating-point addition time was 1.38-1.5 microseconds, multiplication time was 2.48-2.70 microseconds, and division time was 9.00-9.90 microseconds.

Technical impact

While the IBM 7030 was not considered successful, it spawned many technologies incorporated in future machines that were highly successful. The *Standard Modular System* transistor logic was the basis for the IBM 7090 line of scientific computers, the IBM 7070 and 7080 business computers, the IBM 7040 and IBM 1400 lines, and the IBM 1620 small scientific computer. (The 7030 used about 170000 transistors.) The IBM 7302 Model I Core Storage units were also used in the IBM 7090, IBM 7070 and IBM 7080. Multiprogramming, memory protection, generalized interrupts, the 8-bit byte were all concepts later incorporated in the IBM System/360 line of computers as well as most later CPUs. Stephen Dunwell, the project manager who became a scapegoat when Stretch failed commercially, pointed out soon after the phenomenally successful 1964 launch of System/360 that most of its core concepts were pioneered by Stretch.[1] By 1966 he had received an apology and been made an IBM Fellow, a high honor that carried with it resources and authority to pursue one's desired research.[1] Instruction pipelining, prefetch and decoding, and memory interleaving were used in later supercomputer designs such as the IBM System/360 Models 91, 95 and IBM System/370 Model 195, and the IBM 3090 series as well as computers from other manufacturers. As of 2011, these techniques are still used in most advanced microprocessors starting with the Intel

Pentium and the Motorola/IBM PowerPC, as well as in many embedded microprocessors and microcontrollers from various manufacturers.

Customer deliveries

1. Los Alamos Scientific Laboratory (LASL) in April 1961, accepted in May 1961, and used until June 21, 1971.
2. U.S. National Security Agency in February 1962 as the main CPU of the IBM 7950 Harvest system, used until 1976, when the IBM 7955 Tractor tape system developed problems due to worn cams that could not be replaced.
3. Lawrence Livermore Laboratory, Livermore, California.
4. Atomic Weapons Establishment, Aldermaston, England.
5. U.S. Weather Bureau.
6. MITRE Corporation, used until August 1971. In the spring of 1972, it was sold to Brigham Young University.
7. U.S. Navy Dahlgren Naval Proving Ground.
8. IBM.
9. Commissariat à l'énergie atomique, France.

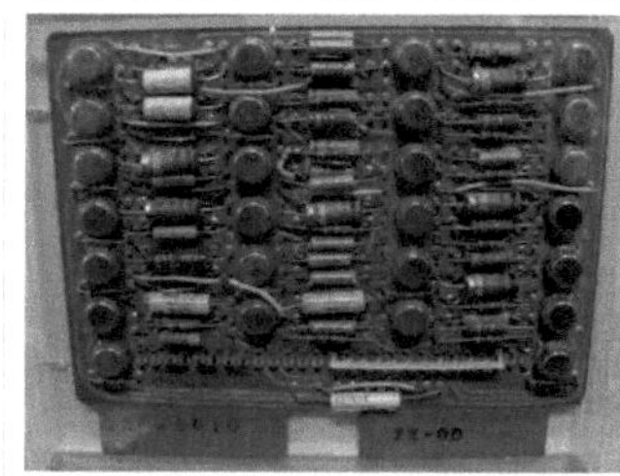

A circuit board from the IBM 7030, in the Bradbury Science Museum, Los Alamos, New Mexico.

The Lawrence Livermore Laboratory's IBM 7030 (except for its core memory) and portions of the MITRE Corporation/Brigham Young University IBM 7030 now reside in the Computer History Museum collection, in Mountain View, California.

Architecture

Data formats

- Fixed point numbers were variable length, stored in either binary (1 to 64 bits) or decimal (1 to 16 digits) and either unsigned format or sign/magnitude format. In decimal format, digits were variable length "bytes" (4 to 8 bits).
- Floating point numbers had a 1-bit exponent flag, a 10-bit exponent, a 1-bit exponent sign, a 48-bit magnitude, and a 4-bit sign "byte" in sign/magnitude format.
- Alphanumeric characters were variable length and could use any character code of 8-bits or less.
- "Bytes" were variable length (1 to 8 bits).

Instruction format

Instructions were either 32-bit or 64-bit.

Registers

The registers overlaid the first 32 addresses of memory, as shown in the table below.

Address	Mnemonic	Register	Stored in:
0	$Z	64-bit Zero	Main Core Storage
1	$IT	19-bit Interval Timer	Index Core Storage
	$TC	36-bit Time Clock	
2	$IA	18-bit Interruption Address	Main Core Storage
3	$UB	18-bit Upper Boundary Address	Transistor Register
	$LB	18-bit Lower Boundary Address	
		1-bit Boundary Control	
4		64-bit Maintenance Bits	Main Core Storage
5	$CA	7-bit Channel Address	Transistor Register
6	$CPUS	19-bit Other CPU Bits	Transistor Register
7	$LZC	7-bit Left Zero count	Transistor Register
	$AOC	7-bit All Ones count	
8	$L	Left half of 128-bit Accumulator	Transistor Register
9	$R	Right half of 128-bit Accumulator	
10	$SB	8-bit Accumulator sign - **ZZZZSTUV**	
11	$IND	64-bit Indicator Register	Transistor Register
12	$MASK	64-bit Mask Register	Transistor Register
13	$RM	64-bit Remainder Register	Main Core Storage
14	$FT	64-bit Factor Register	Main Core Storage
15	$TR	64-bit Transit Register	Main Core Storage
16 ... 31	$X0 ... $X15	64-bit Index Registers (sixteen)	Index Core Storage

The accumulator and Index registers operated in sign-and-magnitude format.

Memory

Main memory was 16K to 256K 64-bit binary words, in banks of 16K.

The memory was immersion oil-heated/cooled to stabilize its operating characteristics.

Software

- STRETCH Assembly Program (STRAP)

See also

- IBM 608, the first commercially available transistorized computing device

References

[1] Simmons & Elsberry 1988, p. 160.

Bibliography

- Simmons, William W.; Elsberry, Richard B. (1988), *Inside IBM: the Watson years (a personal memoir)* (http:// books.google.com/books?vid=ISBN0805931163), Pennsylvania, USA: Dorrance, ISBN 978-0805931167. *The memoir of a senior IBM executive, giving his recollections of his and IBM's experience from World War II into the 1970s.*

External links

- Oral history interview with Gene Amdahl (http://purl.umn.edu/104341) Charles Babbage Institute, University of Minnesota, Minneapolis. Amdahl discusses his role in the design of several computers for IBM including the STRETCH, IBM 701, 701A, and IBM 704. He discusses his work with Nathaniel Rochester and IBM's management of the design process for computers.
- IBM Stretch Collections @ Computer History Museum (http://www.computerhistory.org/collections/ ibmstretch/)
    - Collection index page (http://archive.computerhistory.org/resources/text/IBM/Stretch/pdfs/index.html)
- 7030 Data Processing System (http://www-1.ibm.com/ibm/history/exhibits/mainframe/mainframe_PP7030. html) (IBM Archives)
- IBM Stretch (aka IBM 7030 Data Processing System) (http://www.brouhaha.com/~eric/retrocomputing/ibm/ stretch/)
- Organization Sketch of IBM Stretch (http://cyclone.cs.clemson.edu/~mark/stretch.html)
- BRL report on the IBM Stretch (http://ed-thelen.org/comp-hist/BRL61-ibm7070.html#IBM-STRETCH)
- *Planning a Computer System - Project Stretch* — 1962 book.
    - Scan of copy autographed by several of the contributors (http://ed-thelen.org/comp-hist/ IBM-7030-Planning-McJones.pdf)
    - Searchable PDF file (http://archive.computerhistory.org/resources/text/IBM/Stretch/pdfs/ Buchholz_102636426.pdf)
- IBM 7030 documents at Bitsavers.org (http://www.bitsavers.org/pdf/ibm/7030/) (PDF files)

Article Sources and Contributors

Computer_Usage_Company *Source*: http://en.wikipedia.org/w/index.php?title=Computer_Usage_Company *Contributors*: Decltype, FlashSheridan, Harper3505, Michael Hardy, Paul A, Rjwilmsi, Thom2729, Truthanado, W Nowicki

Software *Source*: http://en.wikipedia.org/w/index.php?title=Software *Contributors*: 021-adilk, 12dstring, 16@r, 194.237.150.xxx, A Stop at Willoughby, A.K.R., ABC1A1, ABF, ALargeElk, AManWithNoPlan, Aardvarkzz, Aatayyab, Abby, Abufaisal65, Achowat, Acroterion, Addshore, Ademsaykin, AdjustShift, Adriancjr, Ah2190, Ahadrt, Ahoerstemeier, AlMac, Alan012, Alansohn, Alasdair, Alazlogexi, Aleemqureshi, Ali K, AlisonW, AlistairMcMillan, Allen4names, Allens, Allmightyduck, Alphachimp, Amalhotra124, Anabus, Andre Engels, Andrea105, Andreas Kaufmann, Andrejj, Andrewspencer, Angela, Angela 2502, Anikingos, Ankur 360, Antandrus, Aoratos, Ap, Apparition11, Aqeelbilal, ArchonMagnus, ArglebargleIV, Arkrishna, Arman Cagle, Arnabatcal, Artichoker, Ashawley, Asiananimal, AuburnPilot, AussieLegend, Autocratique, Avono, Aweiredguy, Axcelis555, AznBurger, BD2412, Backslash Forwardslash, Bact, BalderV, Barek, Bean2thousand, Bearly541, Ben-Zin, Betterusername, Bevo, Big Bird, Big milsy, BigDunc, Binary TSO, Blarrgy, Bobo192, Bonadea, Bongwarrior, Booyabazooka, Boriszex, Boxplot, Brat32, Brent Gulanowski, Brinnington, Brucevdk, Brusegadi, Bryan Derksen, Bubba73, Burnisk, Butros, CIreland, CWenger, Calcifero, Caliboboo1, Can't sleep, clown will eat me, CanadianLinuxUser, Canaima, Canterbury Tail, Cargils02, Carl007, Casperdog2227, Catgut, Causa sui, Cburress, Centrx, Chealer, Christian List, Christian75, Chun-hian, Chuunen Baka, Chzz, Citypanther, Cloudyed, Clovis Sangrail, CommonsDelinker, Conan, Conversion script, CoolD, Coolcaesar, Cpl Syx, Crazykr, Crossmr, Cst17, Cunya, Cyberstrike3000X, Cyrius, DARTH SIDIOUS 2, DBHunter, DJ Clayworth, DLMahnken, DSP-user, DURWHAT, DVdm, Damian Yerrick, Dan Fuhry, Dan100, Danakil, Daniel5127, DanielEng, Darkevilfairy, Darrendeng, Darth Panda, Dave6, Davennmarr, Daveydweeb, DavidWBrooks, Davie4125, Dayewalker, Dbstommy, DeadEyeArrow, Deggalega, Delirium, Denny, DerHexer, Derek farn, Dethme0w, Dffgd, Dibcom, Dina, Dinhtuydzao, Discospinster, Dispenser, DivineAlpha, Dj stone, DmitTrix, Dominator09, Doriftu, Dougofborg, Drawnman247, Dreamatalana, Drewster1829, Drmies, Dugmn, Dwayne, Dycedarg, Dynix, E. Sn0 =31337=, E2eamon, EdBever, Edcolins, Edderso, Edivorce, Edlin, Eeekster, Egbsystem, Ehheh, Eidetic Man, ElBenevolente, Elizium23, Ellenaz, Emana, Emvn, Entropy, Epbr123, Equendil, Erdal Ronahi, EricWesBrown, Esoteric Rogue, Ethine, Everyking, Ex-dot, Excirial, Ezubaric, FJPB, Fang Aili, Fastily, Favonian, Fazilati, Fctk, Feedmecereal, Felyza, Fenice, Fern80, Ff1959, Flarn2006, Flash man999, Flipjargendy, Flubeca, FlyingToaster, Frap, Fratrep, Fred Bradstadt, Fredrik, Fredtheflyingfrog, Freeeeeesoft, Friday, Frip1000, Frosted14, Fubar Obfusco, Funnysens, Fyyer, GDallimore, GSCC, GTBacchus, Gabecuevas, Gadfium, Gaius Cornelius, Galoubet, Gardar Rurak, Gary King, Gazpacho, Geneb1955, Georgia guy, Gfoley4, Giftlite, GilbertoSilvaFan, Gilliam, Ginsengbomb, Gogo Dodo, Gordmoo, Grafen, Greenrd, GregorB, Gronky, Gtg204y, Guanaco, Gueldenberg, Guppy, Gurch, Gwernol, Hadal, Hamiltøn, Hans Dunkelberg, Happyisenough, Harry, Harvester, Hauberk, Haunting The Better, Hayabusa future, Hectorthebat, Hello32020, Hellosandimas, HenryLi, Hmains, Hmcnally, Hno3, Howdoesthiswo, Howling wolf of the jungle, Hu12, Hutcher, Hydrogen Iodide, Icaims, Ifftikhaarrr, Iknowyourider, Imnotminkus, Imroy, IngerAlHaosului, Instinct, Intelligentsium, Into The Fray, Iridescent, Ishara665g, Itsmine, Ixfd64, J Di, J. Spencer, J.delanoy, JLaTondre, JMetzler, Jaan513, Jackaranga, Jacob.jose, Jacqueline7894y, Jam2k, Jamesiemiller, Jan1nad, January, Japonca, Jarda-wien, Jasper Deng, Jay, Jcrwaford5, Jcuadros, Jcw69, Jeff G., Jehochman, Jennapresley, Jeremy Visser, JeremyA, JesseW, Jester7777, Jh51681, Jiang, Jiddisch, Jim1138, Jiy, Jmabel, JoanneB, Johan1298, JohnCD, JonHarder, Jonnabuz, Jop, JordoCo, Joy, Jpbowen, Jpgordon, Jreferee, Jsheadixon, Jtalledo, Jtbatalla, Jusdafax, Jusjih, Justin Eiler, Jóna Þórunn, K.Nevelsteen, K.lee, KFP, KGasso, Kajasudhakarababu, Karol Langner, Kathmandu2007, Kc03, Keilana, Kelldall, Kelly Martin, Kenny sh, Kenyon, KevinCuddeback, Kingpin13, Kinneyboy90, Klilidiplomus, Knodir, Knownot, Knucmo2, Koavf, Kornxi, Kostisl, Kozuch, KrakatoaKatie, Krawi, Ktanzer, Kuldeep06march, Kumioko (renamed), Kurowoofwoof111, Kuru, L Kensington, La Pianista, La comadreja, Labscientist, Lagalag, LaggedOnUser, Lajpatdhingra, Landroo, Lareina3656y, LauriO, Leandro, LeoNomis, Liao, Liberty Miller, Liftarn, Ligulem, LilHelpa, LinDrug, Lindberg G Williams Jr, Listlist, LittleOldMe, Livajo, Lookingchris, Lucianob, Luk, Luna Santin, Lunaumbrax, Luntrasul, Lupo, M4gnum0n, MC10, MD66, MER-C, Macy, Majorbrainy, Malcolm Farmer, Malcolma, Mandarax, Manik762007, Manionc, Manishgoyal.indian, Maralia, Marcelnache, Marek69, MarioS, Markaci, Markwaugh117, Martarius, Master&Expert, Matt Britt, Matt j fox, Matthias M., Matusz, Mav, Maximaximax, Maximus Rex, Mayur, Mcdonald.ross5, Mdd, Mdebets, MeekSaffron, Meelar, Mendalus, Mentifisto, Mermaid from the Baltic Sea, Message From Xenu, Mgrand, Michael Drüing, Michael Hardy, Michal Jurosz, Miguel.mateo, Milan Keršláger, Mild Bill Hiccup, Mindmatrix, Mindspillage, Minesweeper, Minghong, Mini-Geek, Miquonranger03, MithrandirAgain, Mjchonoles, Mkdw, Monobi, Mpete510, Mr Barndoor, MrDKing, MrDolomite, MrOllie, Muffhen, Murray Langton, Mwanner, Mwilso24, Mxn, Myanw, N n abc123, Nabeth, Naik5abhi, Nanshu, Narayana vvss, Nascar1996, Nathanielrichards, Navstar, NawlinWiki, Nbarth, Neil916, Neurophyre, Nharipra, Nick Number, Nickels360, Nikai, Nike8, Nima1024, NinjaCross, Nixdorf, Nixeagle, Nk, Nmrd, Normxxx, Northamerica1000, Nosferatus2007, Nourybouraqadi, Nsaa, NuclearWarfare, Nunquam Dormio, NurAzije, Nurg, Ocaasi, Oda Mari, Ohnoitsjamie, Oicumayberight, Old Moonraker, Oldwes, Oleg Alexandrov, Oliver Lineham, Omicronpersei8, One more night, OrgasGirl, Oxymoron83, P.deshmukh09, P99am, PEH2, PIrish, Page Up, Paranoid, Park3r, Party, Passargea, Paul August, Paul Foxworthy, Paul Niquette, Pcap, PeaceAnywhere, Perkinsleslie, Peruvianllama, Peter Winnberg, Petrb, Pgk, Pgr94, Phatom87, PhilHibbs, PhilKnight, Philip Howard, Philip Trueman, Phillip Ca, Piano non troppo, Piasa1, Pigduckmeatshroom, Pilotguy, Pip2andahalf, Pnm, Poccil, Pohatu771, Pointillist, Poo1000, Pooryorick, Prahim, Priyadarshi.pratyush, Programmer13, Prohlep, Psantora, Public Menace, Puchiko, Pufferfish101, Puneet1507, Purgatory Fubar, Pyfan, Quinobi, Quinsareth, QuintusQuill, R. S. Shaw, RHaworth, Ragha joshi, Ragib, Rainier3, RainierHa, Rajeshmagic, Random89, Raul654, Ray Van De Walker, Rayhu, Rbreen, Reaper Eternal, Rebroad, Recnilgiarc, Recognizance, RedWolf, Redmercury82, Reedy, Rehnn83, Reisio, Remember the dot, Rettetast, RevRagnarok, Revised, Rgill, Rholton, Rhye123, Riana, Rich Farmbrough, Richard cocks, RickK, Rihannoufal, Ripogenus77, Rl, Rodhullandemu, Rogger.Ferguson, Roland2, Ronhjones, RossPatterson, Roybb95, Rurik, Rwwww, Ryulong, S.K., S0aasdf2sf, SC979, SF007, ST47, SaadTeenager, Sadeq, Sadi Carnot, Safalra, Safarj, Saleem110, Salmank120, Salsa Shark, Sango123, SchfiftyThree, SchreyP, Scientus, Scrool, Seaphoto, Seb az86556, Seidenstud, Senator Palpatine, Setveen, Seven.cardwell, SewerCat, Shadowjams, Shakya ind, Shaluhijas, Siggy28, Sigma 7, Sigondronggondrong, Siliconov, Silivrenion, SimonP, Sintonak.X, Sitarherophil, Sivaguru411, Sjö, Skarebo, Skizzik, Skybon, Slingerjansen, Slowking Man, Slowmo1993, Smack, Smalljim, Snowmanradio, Sokrato, Soler97, Some jerk on the Internet, Sorryranga94, South Bay, Speaksleft, Spectrogram, Spoon!, SpuriousQ, Standalone0109, Starkiller88, Stephenb, SteveWringsfield, Steven Zhang, Stewartadcock, StuffOfInterest, SudoGhost, Supadawg, Super-Magician, Supersteve04038, Suruena, SusanLesch, SwirlBoy39, Syrthiss, T, T3h 1337 b0y, T4tarzan, TC Cannon, THEN WHO WAS PHONE?, TPK, TaintedMustard, Tangent747, Tasja, TastyPoutine, Tbhotch, Tejas81, Teles, Teryan2006, Th1rt3en, Tharcore, The Anome, The Earwig, The High Fin Sperm Whale, The Rambling Man, The Thing That Should Not Be, The Transhumanist (AWB), TheBiaatch, Thelb4, Thingg, This acccount is a vandalism, Thumperward, Thurak13, Tide rolls, Tiffu, Tigershrike, Tim Q. Wells, Timhowardriley, Timothy Neilen, Tommy2010, Topbanana, Torc2, Torinor, Traroth, Trevor MacInnis, Triona, Triwbe, True Genius, Trueshow111, Trusilver, Turlo Lomon, Tuxide, Twsx, Uncle Milty, Unyoyega, Uriyan, Utuado, Vale Len, Vbigdeli, Velella, Venkisree, Versageek, Versus22, Vibhijain, Virtualenv, Virtualsfera, Viskonsas, Vrenator, W Nowicki, WLU, Wavelength, Wayne Slam, Wayward, Wbm1058, Web20image, Werdna, Weregerbil, Wernher, Wexhammer, Weyes, Whitew123, Wiki alf, Wikicrazier2011, Wikidudeman, Wikieditor06, Wikijens, Wimt, Winterst, Wireless friend, Wm, WojPob, Woohookitty, WookieInHeat, Wshun, Wysprgr2005, XP1, Xdenizen, Xevious, Xionbox, Xplodercop, Yamamoto Ichiro, Yasirilyas, Yidisheryid, Yoooder, YountLor, Yworo, Zarkos, Zatya34, Zedlik, ZeroOne, Zerokewl, Zhou Yu, ZimZalaBim, Zybez, Александър, Евгени Симеонов, Петър Петров, ТимофейЛееСуда, 1844 anonymous edits

Federal_Aviation_Administration *Source*: http://en.wikipedia.org/w/index.php?title=Federal_Aviation_Administration *Contributors*: 0x6D667061, 2T, 7, Ace of Spades, Acxiz, Ageekgal, Ahunt, Airplaneman, Akradecki, Alborzagros, Allstargold, Apparition11, Aris Katsaris, Artcort.fis, AuburnPilot, Awg1010, Beland, Bender235, Benvogel, BilCat, Bookandcoffee, Briaboru, Bsimmons666, CAMIOKC, CambridgeBayWeather, Can't sleep, clown will eat me, CapitalR, Capitalstroadster, Ceradon, Check-Six, Cleared as filed, Clindberg, ConradKilroy, Conversion script, CopperSquare, Covalent, Crum375, DS Riley, Dan Dassow, Darkwind, Dave English, David.Monniaux, DeeJaye6, Deejaye6, Dwight Burdette, Eastlaw, Emote, Epbr123, Epolk, Eric-Wester, Erpel13, Faa dude, Faaregulations, Falphin, Fanatix, Flyguy33, Franamax, Funandtrvl, GD 6041, Galoubet, Gautamgk, Gbbinning, Gcapp1959, Glenn, GoldRingChip, Graham87, Grant76, Hervegirod, HiB2Bornot2B, Highfly3442, I Love Pi, Ian Spackman, Iancarter, Ida Shaw, Iridescent, Jan Pospíšil, Japanese Searobin, Jayman20ja, Jef-Infojef, Jhf, Jkneps63, JohnWhitlock, Johnpacklambert, JonHarder, Jross.hfdesign, Jtm711, Jusdafax, Justfred, Justinwerden, Jwolcott77, Ketiltrout, KinsmanRedeemer, Ksyrie, Kusma, Leslie Mateus, Levineps, Lexw, Life, Liberty, Property, Lindbergh2002, Lnuss, Lotje, Lrduncan, MBisanz, Mahjongg, Manco Capac, Marrante, Mattbrundage, Meekywiki, Michael Hardy, Miketwo, Million Little Gods, Mindmatrix, Minna Sora no Shita, Misterrick, Mlturro, Ms2ger, Mulad, Nathan Johnson, Neutrality, Ng.j, Noommos, Novum, Numerousfalx, OMenda, OWL, Ohnoitsjamie, Oxymoron83, PaulHanson, Pauly04, Pearle, Perfectblue97, Petersam, Postdlf, Quebec99, Quercus basaseachicensis, RandomP, Rcknight, Reedy, Requestion, Richard Weil, Richard cocks, Rjd0060, Rjwilmsi, Rlandmann, Rob38204, Romney yw, Rougher07, Rrekn, Rsrikanth05, RussBlau, Russavia, S h i v a (noni), SNIyer12, Saa.caas, Sam, Sardanaphalus, SarekOfVulcan, Scott5114, Seth Goldin, Shadowjams, Shanew2, Shellbell, SiegeLord, Signortgel, SimonP, Simone, Skeppy, Soucdb, Sperril, Spondoolicks, Stephen Gilbert, Sukee3, Sumsum2010, SuzanneIAM, T18, Taestell, Tarrow, Tassedethe, Template namespace initialisation script, The Founders Intent, Thewinchester, Tofutwitch11, TommyBoy, Treesmill, V-two, VeggieGarden, Vircotto, Vots, Welsh, Wereon, WhisperToMe, Wikiacc, Wikip rhyre, Wikipelli, Wikispork, Yuriybrisk, Zoicon5, ZooCrewMan, 197 anonymous edits

National_Aviation_Facilities_Experimental_Center *Source*: http://en.wikipedia.org/w/index.php?title=National_Aviation_Facilities_Experimental_Center *Contributors*: Dv82matt, Johnpacklambert, Jross.hfdesign, KConWiki, Malcolma, S. M. Sullivan, W Nowicki

IBM_650 *Source*: http://en.wikipedia.org/w/index.php?title=IBM_650 *Contributors*: Alkivar, Andreas Sons, Arjun G. Menon, ArnoldReinhold, AttishOculus, Beagle84, Brouhaha, Bubba73, Bumm13, Chatul, Chzz, Clemente, David Kubin, Dmsar, Gene Nygaard, Gortu, Greensburger, Gunter, Hede2000, Hmains, Jerome Charles Potts, Jpaulm, Mfc, Oneiros, Philcha, Quota, R.123, RTC, Ray Van De Walker, Rich Farmbrough, Rjwilmsi, Rwwww, SHeumann, Sdegiorg, Sstrader, Stepho-wrs, The Thing That Should Not Be, Updatebjarni, Viznut, Wernher, WhiteDragon, 60 anonymous edits

Initial_public_offering *Source*: http://en.wikipedia.org/w/index.php?title=Initial_public_offering *Contributors*: 5464536, 7, A.R., Aaron Levy-Forsythe, Ab.er.rant, Ahoerstemeier, Ajelectrowhiz, All-or-none, Alokagga, Altenmann, Andrewpmk, Anticipation of a New Lover's Arrival, The, Art LaPella, Aude, AzadRubel, Azurina, Beagel, Bender235, BesselDekker, Bigoperm, Blazotron, Bluezy, Bombastus, Bongwarrior, Bped1985, Brian Willis, Buddha24, CaliforniaAliBaba, Camw, Chancemill, Cometstyles, Conant Webb, Cretog8, DBigXray, DMCer, Dasickis, David Gale, Debiobbi, Deineka, Deiz, Deli nk, Devanium, Dicklyon, Djaconi, Dkorn, DocendoDiscimus, Dogposter, Dougransom, Dritorii, Duedilly, Ed g2s, Edjerge, Emerybob, Epbr123, Eraserhead1, Ewlyahoocom, Faderrattnerb, Feco, Flowanda, Fredbauder, Fredrik, FreplySpang, Gaius Cornelius, Galatee, Galoubet, Gary King, Gnfnrf, Gsarwa, Hakseng, Hang Li Po, Heavie, Hellomanwaturname, HenryLi, Hmbr, Holden15, Hu12, Hvn0413, Ian Pitchford, Ibesmart, Ida Shaw, Ikiatop10, Isa Roarte, J.delanoy, JJ211219, Jandalhandler, Jarbdpo, Jarble, Jauerback, Jaysweet, Jerryseinfeld, Jerzy, Jewbacca, Jim1138, Johnteslade, Joshua Issac, Jovany rojo, Jphillips, Julesd, JustAGal, KenBest, Kevin McE, Kku, Krazitrain, Krich, Kurtm3, Lakhotiaatul, Lamro, Law-corrector, Leonid Antonenko, Lightmouse, Lootzyne, Lootzynewiki, Lotje, Lycurgus, MER-C, Manop, Manticore, Martinp23, Maurreen, Mehran, MementoVivere,

Meowist, Mic, Michael Hardy, MildInvestor, Minesweeper, Modest Genius, Mordo248, Mr Stephen, Naught101, Navia2011, Ncmvocalist, NeilN, NickW557, Nopetro, NorsemanII, Ohnoitsjamie, Ojay123, Olivier, Onnoysomoy, Pasd, PeepP, Phantomsteve, Philip Trueman, PhilipO, Piano non troppo, Pikappa, Pippin Bear, Platinum Dragon, Pmlineditor, Poccil, Pparazorback, Ppirozzi, Preschooler.at.heart, RainbowOfLight, Rapsar, Rastrelli F, Rdale, Rich Farmbrough, Richard Arthur Norton (1958-), Richie, Rmudambi, Robinth, Rocket71048576, Rolandograndi, Romanc19s, RoyBoy, SEKIUCHI, Seajaylootz, Sean.hoyland, Seaphoto, Secretlondon, Seekingalpha1980, Sekicho, Shadow1, Shadowjams, Shrug-shrug, SilverStar, Simetrical, Skew-t, Skysmith, Slightsmile, Slowking Man, Smallbones, Sowmya mani, Sphayros, Squirepants101, Sridharan.alwar, St.daniel, Stefancina, Strange Passerby, Sybren, TYelliot, TakuyaMurata, TastyPoutine, Taxman, The Thing That Should Not Be, TheObtuseAngleOfDoom, Theilert, Thomas Paine1776, Thumperward, Tiger888, Tinton5, Tnnr, Tommy2010, Tony1, Tonytonytonyk, Tphalter, Tsuji, Ulric1313, Urbanrenewal, Vamsi.chch, Vegas949, Vegaswikian, Venture Capital in Pakistan, Vipul2606, Vrenator, WJetChao, Wall Street CEO, Wangi, War59312, West.andrew.g, Wikidemon, Wikipediarules2221, Wikky Horse, Wk muriithi, Woohookitty, Xionbox, Yflicker, Zhou Yu, Zoz, , 429 anonymous edits

Cuthbert_Hurd *Source*: http://en.wikipedia.org/w/index.php?title=Cuthbert_Hurd *Contributors*: BD2412, Bender235, Dsp13, Erkan Yilmaz, Harper3505, Iridescent, Mdd, Rjwilmsi, So66, Thom2729, Torla42, Valentinejoesmith, W Nowicki, 5 anonymous edits

IBM_System/360 *Source*: http://en.wikipedia.org/w/index.php?title=IBM_System/360 *Contributors*: 62.253.64.xxx, Abba1943, Abcarter, Acdx, Adicarlo, Alai, Alan Larson, Alfie66, Andrew Kanaber, Andrewa, Ap, Apoc2400, Arch dude, ArnoldReinhold, Ashleyandhenna, Austriacus, Avijja, BBCWatcher, BBird, Bachcell, Bart133, BenFranske, Bender235, Bevo, BjKa, BlueH2O, Bovineone, BradBeattie, Brouhaha, Bumm13, Carbuncle, Carmichael, Ccalvin, Chatul, Chealer, Choster, Chowbok, Cogiati, ConradPino, Conversion script, Ctmt, DaleDe, David.Monniaux, Dawynn, Dekimasu, Delcnsltmd, Dick107, Dmsar, Dulciana, Dyl, EagleOne, Elkman, Emperorbma, Erud, Farosdaughter, Funandtrvl, Gah4, Gaius Cornelius, Geo Swan, GioCM, Gioto, GoingBatty, Greensburger, Gunter, Guy Harris, HairyFotr, Harej, Hif, Hmains, Isnow, Iwilcox, JRTessier, Jakew, Jamescfield, Jmchuff, Jnc, John Nevard, John Sauter, John W. Kennedy, Josh Parris, Jph, Jsavit, Juliancumbria, Kubanczyk, KymFarnik, LittleDan, Loadmaster, Lupine Proletariat, MWS, Maccess, Magus732, Mark Triggers, MartinPackerIBM, Maury Markowitz, Mav, Mfc, MilesFrmOrdnary, MileyDavidA, Mo ainm, Monedula, Mushroom, Mvanner, Mwilso24, Naleks, NewEnglandYankee, Nparlante, Nricardo, Nwbeeson, Peter Flass, Peter bertok, PeterJeremy, Peterh5322, Pit, Pnm, Prosebigpond, RTC, Raryel, Reywas92, Rfc1394, Rich Farmbrough, Richiez, Robin400, Rogatien, Rohan Jayasekera, RossPatterson, Ruzulo, Rwalker, Rwwww, SHOlafsson, Samohyl Jan, SaturdayNightSpecial, Shoaler, Spinality, Starsonh, Stepa, Supadawg, Supersquid, T-bonham, Tedickey, Teles, Tempshill, The Anome, Tom94022, Toresbe, UnicornTapestry, Vntgntks, W163, Wa3frp, Wernher, Wikid77, Wikiklrsc, Woohookitty, Wtshymanski, Xanzzibar, Yaronf, , 166 anonymous edits

IBM_7030_Stretch *Source*: http://en.wikipedia.org/w/index.php?title=IBM_7030_Stretch *Contributors*: -Majestic-, A876, Aspects, Bobblewik, Brouhaha, Bubba73, Bumm13, Chzz, Cogiati, David.Monniaux, Dawynn, Deltabeignet, Dicklyon, Dmsar, Doradus, Gennytte, GermanX, Gortu, Guy Harris, Hellisp, Jerome Charles Potts, JohnOwens, Kabads, Kenevans98365, Magus732, Michaelwilson, Miyagawa, Mmernex, Morio, Nick Pisarro, Jr., Nv8200p, Oldfarm, Pcap, Pissant, R. S. Shaw, RTC, Raul654, Ron2, Rwwww, Thom2729, Three-quarter-ten, Timhogs, TonyW, Torla42, Waltgibson, Wernher, Zoicon5, 37 anonymous edits

Image Sources, Licenses and Contributors

Image:Computer Usage Company logo.jpg *Source*: http://en.wikipedia.org/w/index.php?title=File:Computer_Usage_Company_logo.jpg *License*: unknown *Contributors*: W Nowicki

Image:Operating system placement.svg *Source*: http://en.wikipedia.org/w/index.php?title=File:Operating_system_placement.svg *License*: unknown *Contributors*: Photos:GolfthemanGolftheman

file:US-FederalAviationAdmin-Seal.svg *Source*: http://en.wikipedia.org/w/index.php?title=File:US-FederalAviationAdmin-Seal.svg *License*: unknown *Contributors*: U.S. Government

File:DOT-FAA Headquarters by Matthew Bisanz.JPG *Source*: http://en.wikipedia.org/w/index.php?title=File:DOT-FAA_Headquarters_by_Matthew_Bisanz.JPG *License*: unknown *Contributors*: User:MBisanz

Image:FAA Joint Surveillance Site Canton Michigan.JPG *Source*: http://en.wikipedia.org/w/index.php?title=File:FAA_Joint_Surveillance_Site_Canton_Michigan.JPG *License*: unknown *Contributors*: User:Deedeebee

File:IBM 650 at Texas A&M.jpg *Source*: http://en.wikipedia.org/w/index.php?title=File:IBM_650_at_Texas_A&M.jpg *License*: unknown *Contributors*: Cushing Memorial Library and Archives, Texas A&M

Image:IBM-650-panel.jpg *Source*: http://en.wikipedia.org/w/index.php?title=File:IBM-650-panel.jpg *License*: unknown *Contributors*: User:mfc

Image:IBM-650-wiring.jpg *Source*: http://en.wikipedia.org/w/index.php?title=File:IBM-650-wiring.jpg *License*: unknown *Contributors*: User:mfc

Image:IBM 650 EMMA.jpg *Source*: http://en.wikipedia.org/w/index.php?title=File:IBM_650_EMMA.jpg *License*: unknown *Contributors*: User:Mahlum

File:RoehreIBM 090325.jpg *Source*: http://en.wikipedia.org/w/index.php?title=File:RoehreIBM_090325.jpg *License*: unknown *Contributors*: JuergenG

File:BronxScienceProgrammingClassroom1960.jpg *Source*: http://en.wikipedia.org/w/index.php?title=File:BronxScienceProgrammingClassroom1960.jpg *License*: unknown *Contributors*: User:Jsclar

File:Bundesarchiv B 145 Bild-F038812-0014, Wolfsburg, VW Autowerk.jpg *Source*: http://en.wikipedia.org/w/index.php?title=File:Bundesarchiv_B_145_Bild-F038812-0014,_Wolfsburg,_VW_Autowerk.jpg *License*: unknown *Contributors*: Schaack, Lothar

Image:DM IBM S360.jpg *Source*: http://en.wikipedia.org/w/index.php?title=File:DM_IBM_S360.jpg *License*: unknown *Contributors*: Ben Franske

File:IBM System360 Model 30.jpg *Source*: http://en.wikipedia.org/w/index.php?title=File:IBM_System360_Model_30.jpg *License*: unknown *Contributors*: Dave Ross

Image:IBM360-65-1.corestore.jpg *Source*: http://en.wikipedia.org/w/index.php?title=File:IBM360-65-1.corestore.jpg *License*: unknown *Contributors*: Original uploader was ArnoldReinhold at en.wikipedia

File:360-91-panel.jpg *Source*: http://en.wikipedia.org/w/index.php?title=File:360-91-panel.jpg *License*: unknown *Contributors*: Avron, Infrogmation, Mattes, Topory, Toresbe

Image:IBM 360 20 TROS.jpg *Source*: http://en.wikipedia.org/w/index.php?title=File:IBM_360_20_TROS.jpg *License*: unknown *Contributors*: Bulwersator

Image:ChannelConnector.JPG *Source*: http://en.wikipedia.org/w/index.php?title=File:ChannelConnector.JPG *License*: unknown *Contributors*: User:BlueH2O

Image:ChannelTerminator.JPG *Source*: http://en.wikipedia.org/w/index.php?title=File:ChannelTerminator.JPG *License*: unknown *Contributors*: User:BlueH2O

Image:SLT Card Frame.corestore.jpg *Source*: http://en.wikipedia.org/w/index.php?title=File:SLT_Card_Frame.corestore.jpg *License*: unknown *Contributors*: Original uploader was ArnoldReinhold at en.wikipedia

Image:IBM 2311 memory unit.JPG *Source*: http://en.wikipedia.org/w/index.php?title=File:IBM_2311_memory_unit.JPG *License*: unknown *Contributors*: User:Deep silence

File:IBM2314DiskDrivesAndIBM2540CardReaderPunch.jpg *Source*: http://en.wikipedia.org/w/index.php?title=File:IBM2314DiskDrivesAndIBM2540CardReaderPunch.jpg *License*: unknown *Contributors*: Scott Gerstenberger

File:IBM System 360 tape drives.jpg *Source*: http://en.wikipedia.org/w/index.php?title=File:IBM_System_360_tape_drives.jpg *License*: unknown *Contributors*: Erik Pitti from San Diego, CA, USA

Image:IBM line printer 1403.JPG *Source*: http://en.wikipedia.org/w/index.php?title=File:IBM_line_printer_1403.JPG *License*: unknown *Contributors*: waelder

Image:IBM7030 p1040280.jpg *Source*: http://en.wikipedia.org/w/index.php?title=File:IBM7030_p1040280.jpg *License*: unknown *Contributors*: User:David.Monniaux

Image:IBM7030 p1040281.jpg *Source*: http://en.wikipedia.org/w/index.php?title=File:IBM7030_p1040281.jpg *License*: unknown *Contributors*: User:David.Monniaux

File:IBM 7030 Stretch circuit board.jpg *Source*: http://en.wikipedia.org/w/index.php?title=File:IBM_7030_Stretch_circuit_board.jpg *License*: unknown *Contributors*: Mark Pellegrini

Printed by Books on Demand GmbH, Norderstedt / Germany